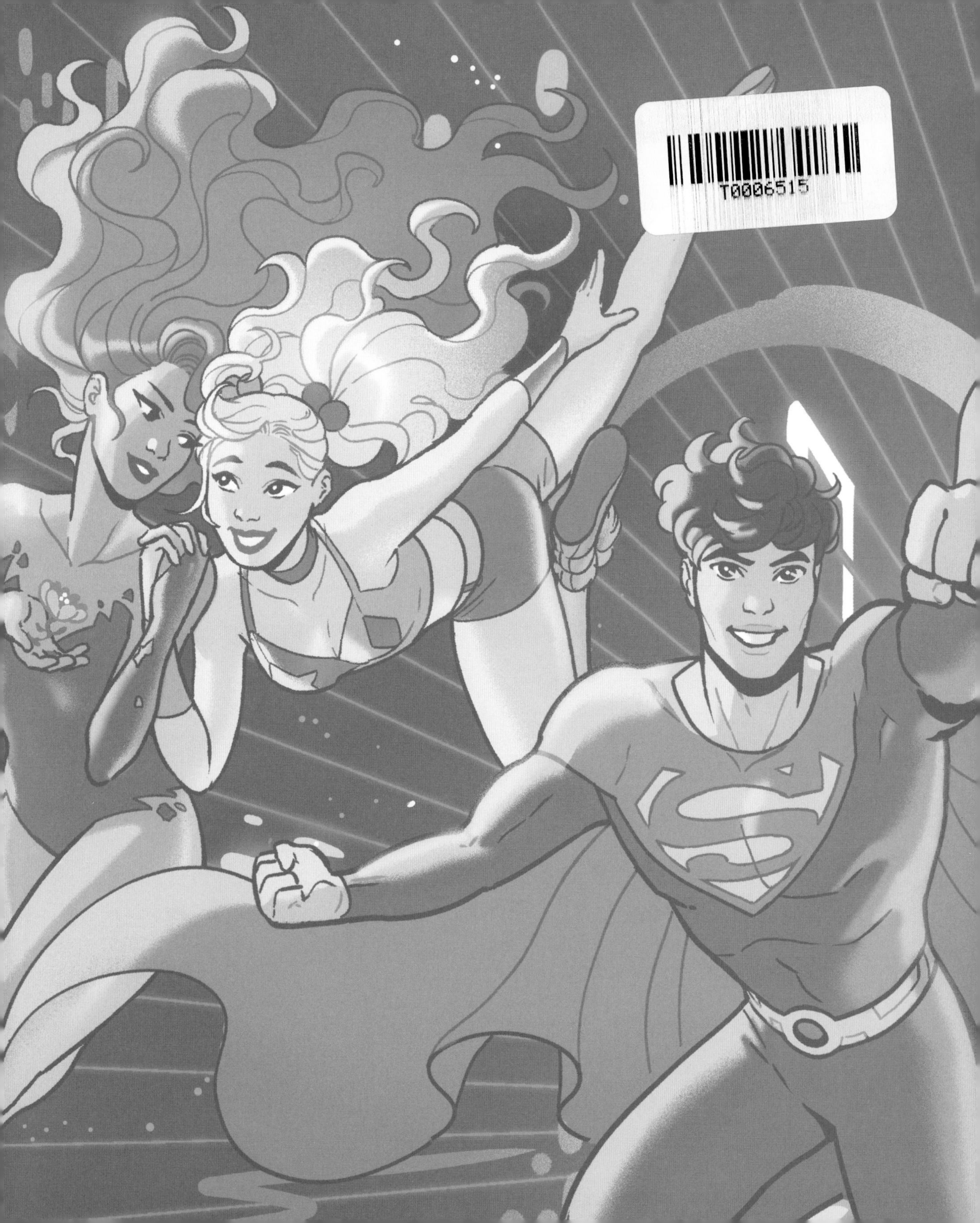

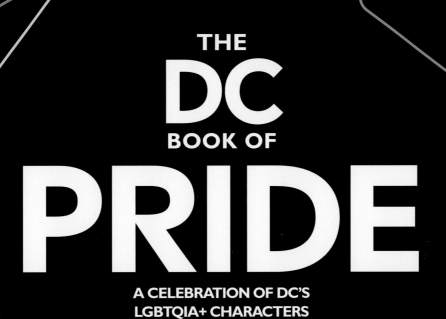

THE
DC
BOOK OF
PRIDE

**A CELEBRATION OF DC'S
LGBTQIA+ CHARACTERS**

THE
DC
BOOK OF
PRIDE

A CELEBRATION OF DC'S
LGBTQIA+ CHARACTERS

WRITTEN BY
JADZIA AXELROD

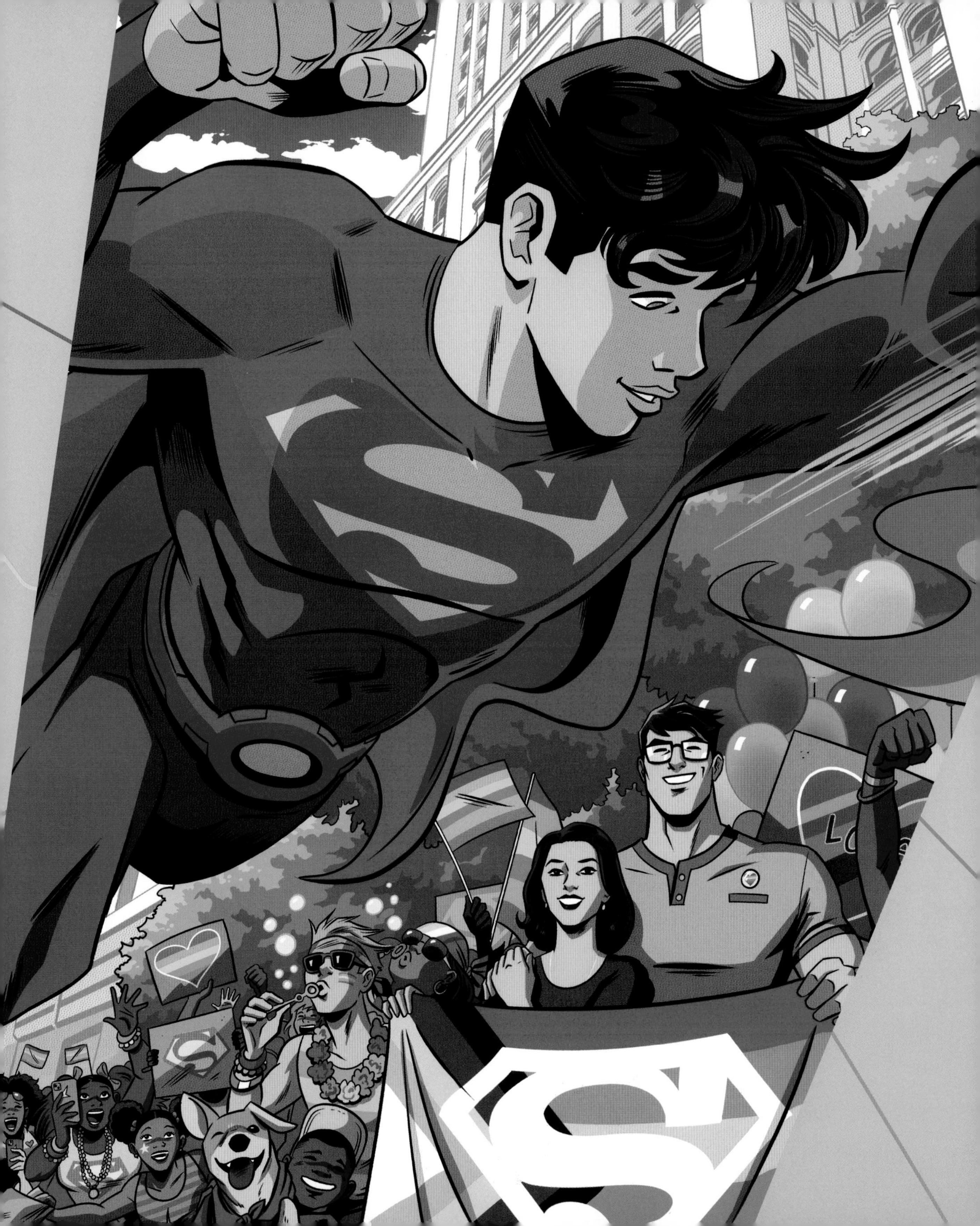

CONTENTS

INTRODUCTION 8

THE AERIE 10
ALYSIA YEOH 12
APOLLO 14
AQUAMAN (JACKSON HYDE) 16
ARTEMIS 18
ARUNA SHENDE 20
BATWOMAN (KATE KANE) 22
BIA 24
BLUE SNOWMAN 26
BLUEBIRD 28
BUNKER 30
CATMAN 32
THE CHEETAH (BARBARA MINERVA) 34
CIRCUIT BREAKER 36
COAGULA 38
CRUSH 40
DREAMER 42
ETTA CANDY 44
EXTRAÑO 46
THE FLASH (JESS CHAMBERS) 48
GALAXY 50
GHOST-MAKER 52
GRACE CHOI 54
GREEN ARROW (CONNOR HAWKE) 56
GREEN LANTERN (ALAN SCOTT) 58
GREEN LANTERN (SOJOURNER MULLEIN) 60
HARLEY QUINN 62
HIPPOLYTA 64
HOLLY ROBINSON 66
IO 68
JAY NAKAMURA 70
JERICHO 72

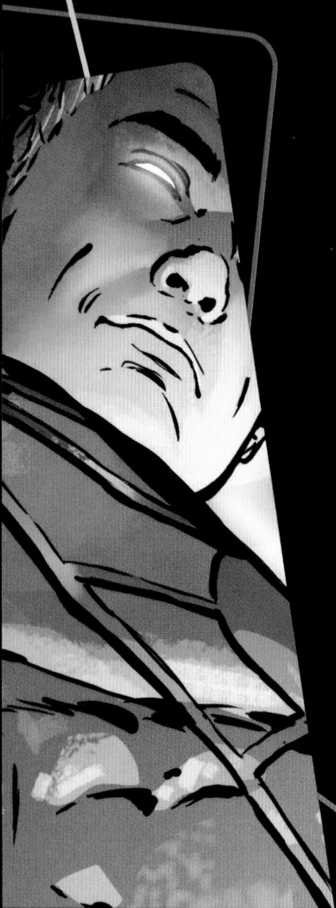

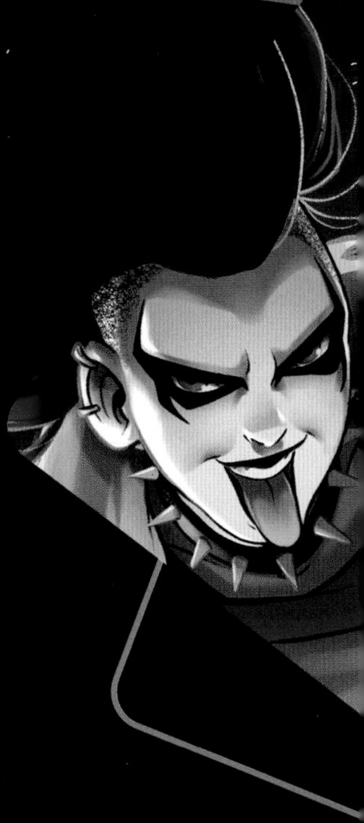

A NOTE ON THE DATA FILES

Across the vast and ever-expanding DC universe, there are many different iterations of these beloved characters. In this book, each entry's data file contains the first appearance of this specific version of the character.

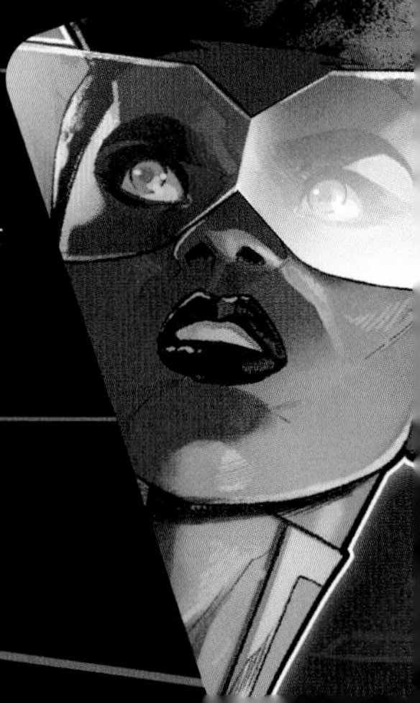

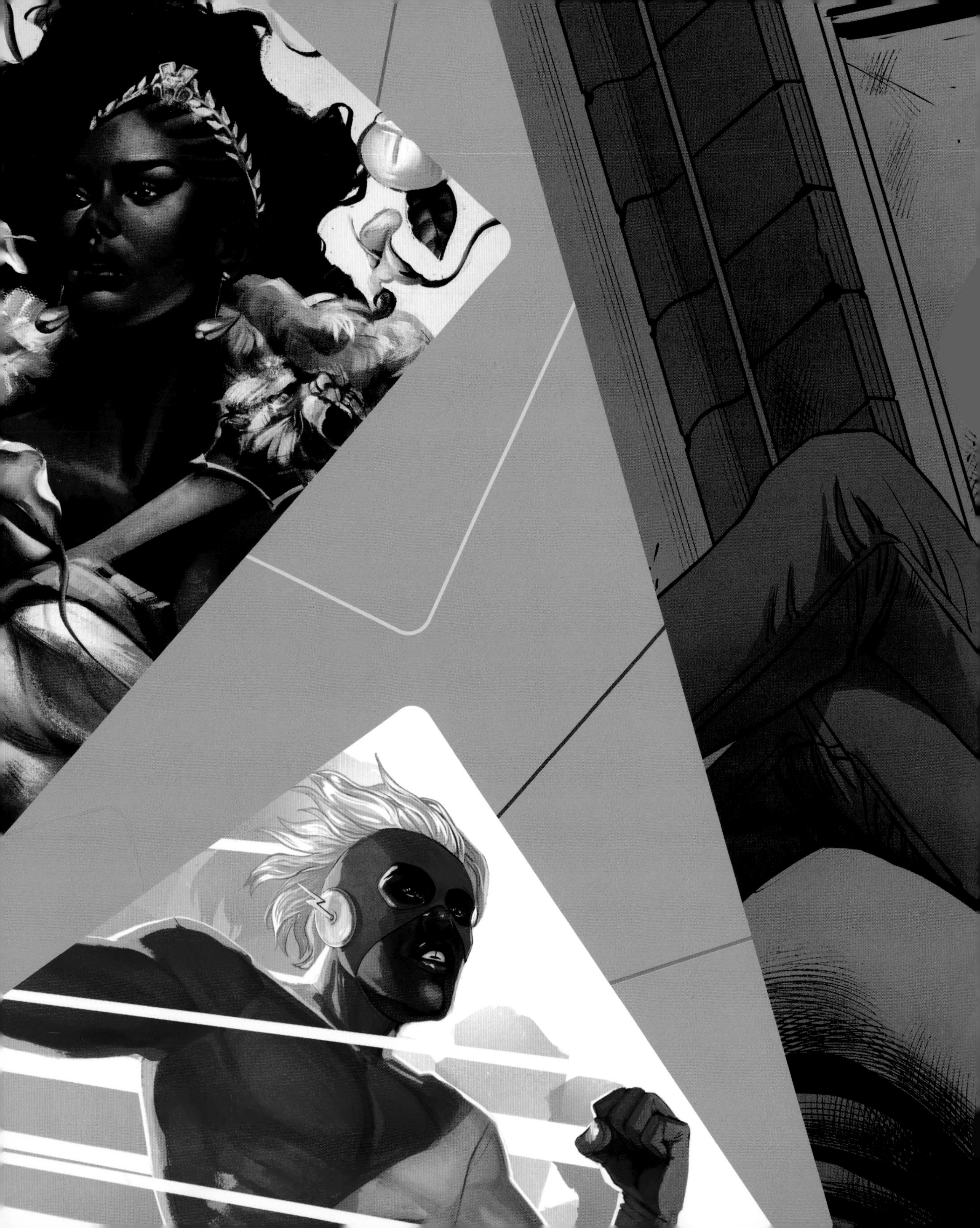

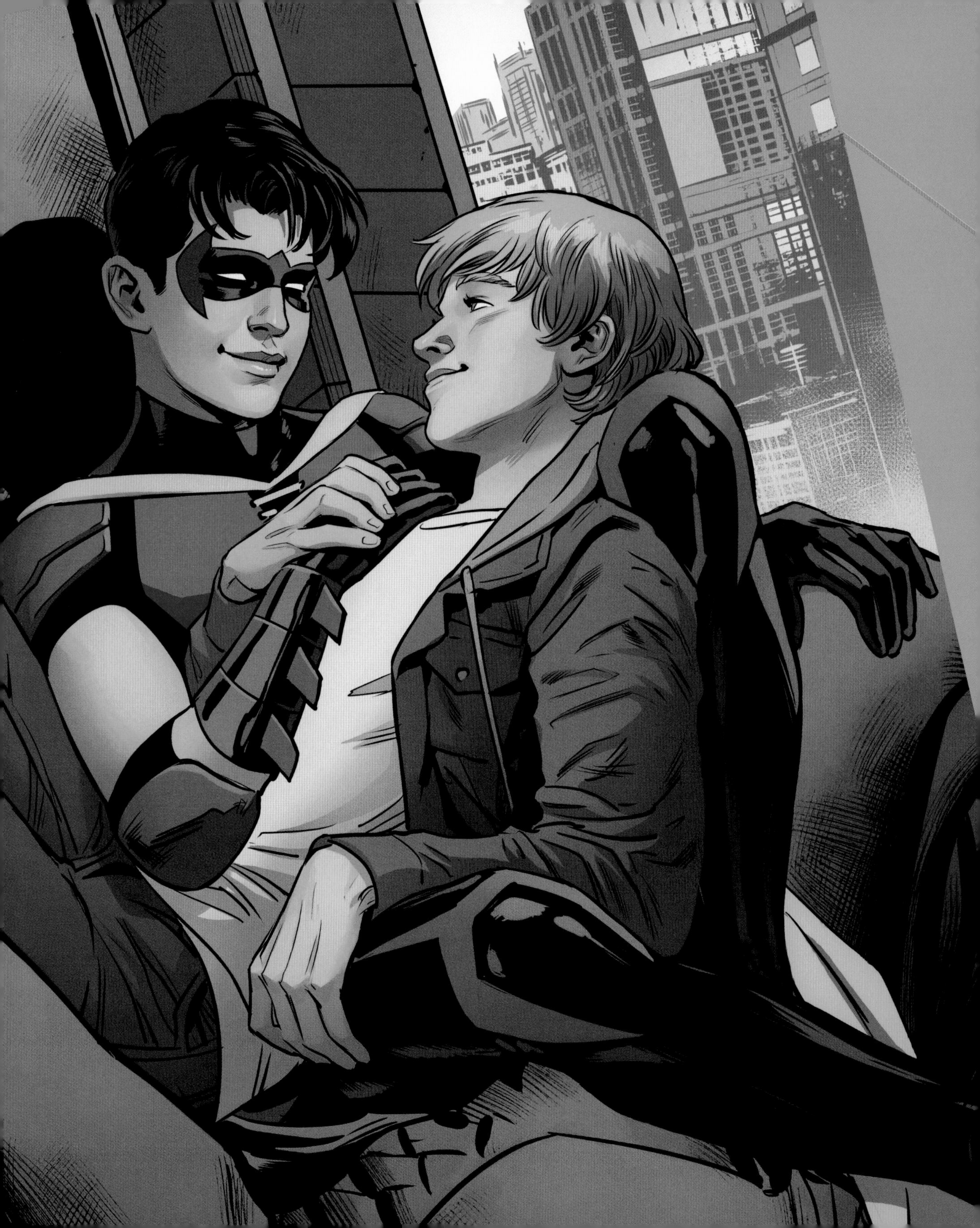

INTRODUCTION

While researching this book, I was staggered by the number of LGBTQIA+ characters in the DC universe. There are *hundreds*. I didn't expect that.

The reason I was surprised was the Comics Code Authority. The CCA began in 1954, a regulatory organization created to combat a perception that comics had become too violent, too lurid. Among the prohibitions of the CCA was any and all representation of queerness. No queer characters. At all.

And yet, there they were. Brave characters brought to life by even braver creative teams. Their sexuality had to be hinted at instead of declared outright, but they existed. Some are heroes, some are villains, but very few of them were leads. Most of them get their stories told with a wink and a coded inference, supporting the straight characters whose name is in the title. A pantheon of gods and mortals, paragons and despots, and ordinary people, showcasing all the shades of the rainbow.

Since DC's abandonment of the CCA, queer characters have been able to show their loves, lives, and losses on-panel in glorious detail. They've gotten to have their names on the titles, leads in their own stories. Today's LGBTQIA+ characters can be themselves with pride.

They couldn't all fit in this book. But this book was never intended to be an exhaustive list. Instead, think of it as an introduction, a celebration. My hope is you will be inspired by the characters within and seek out the others. There are so, so many, and they all deserve to have their stories told.

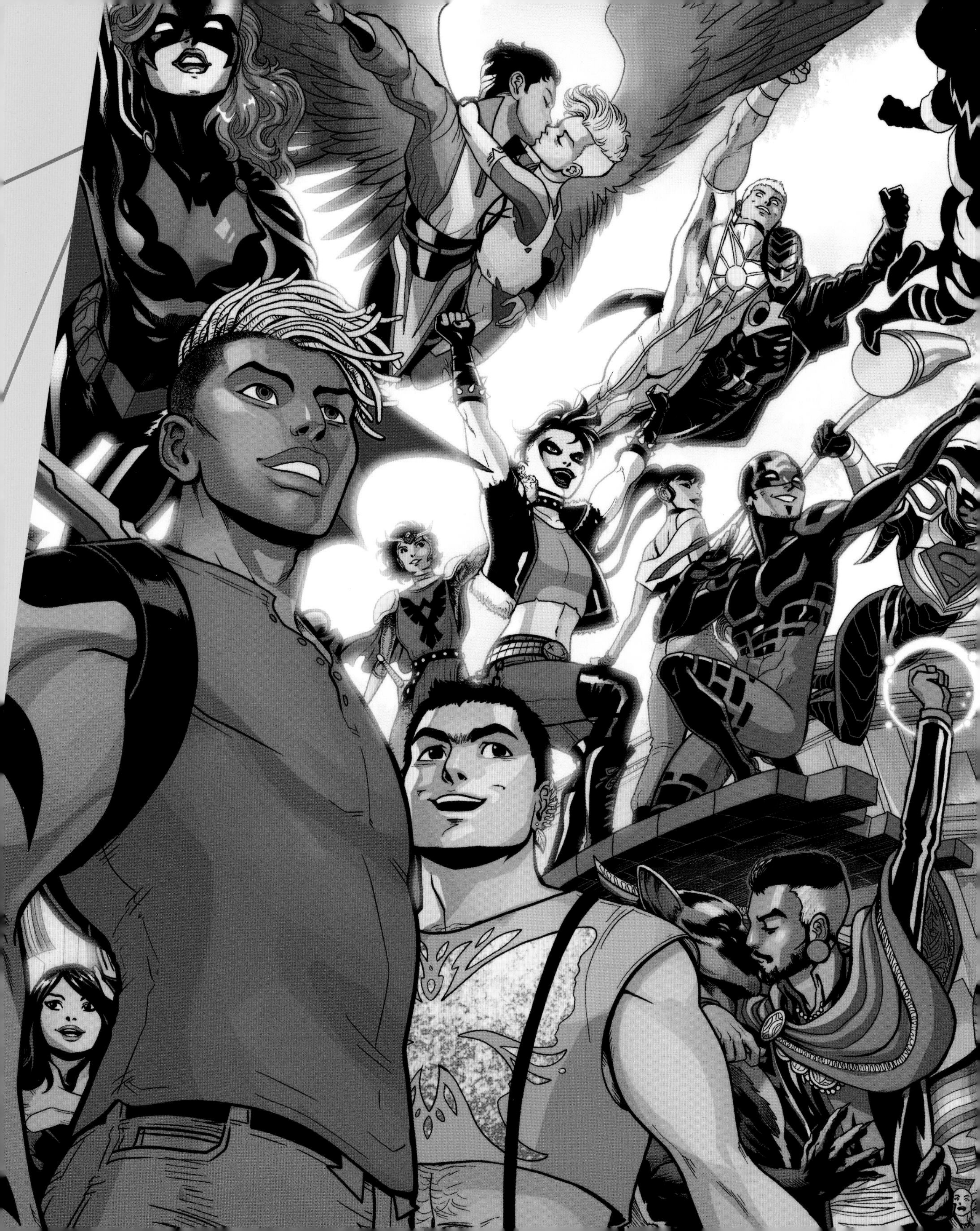

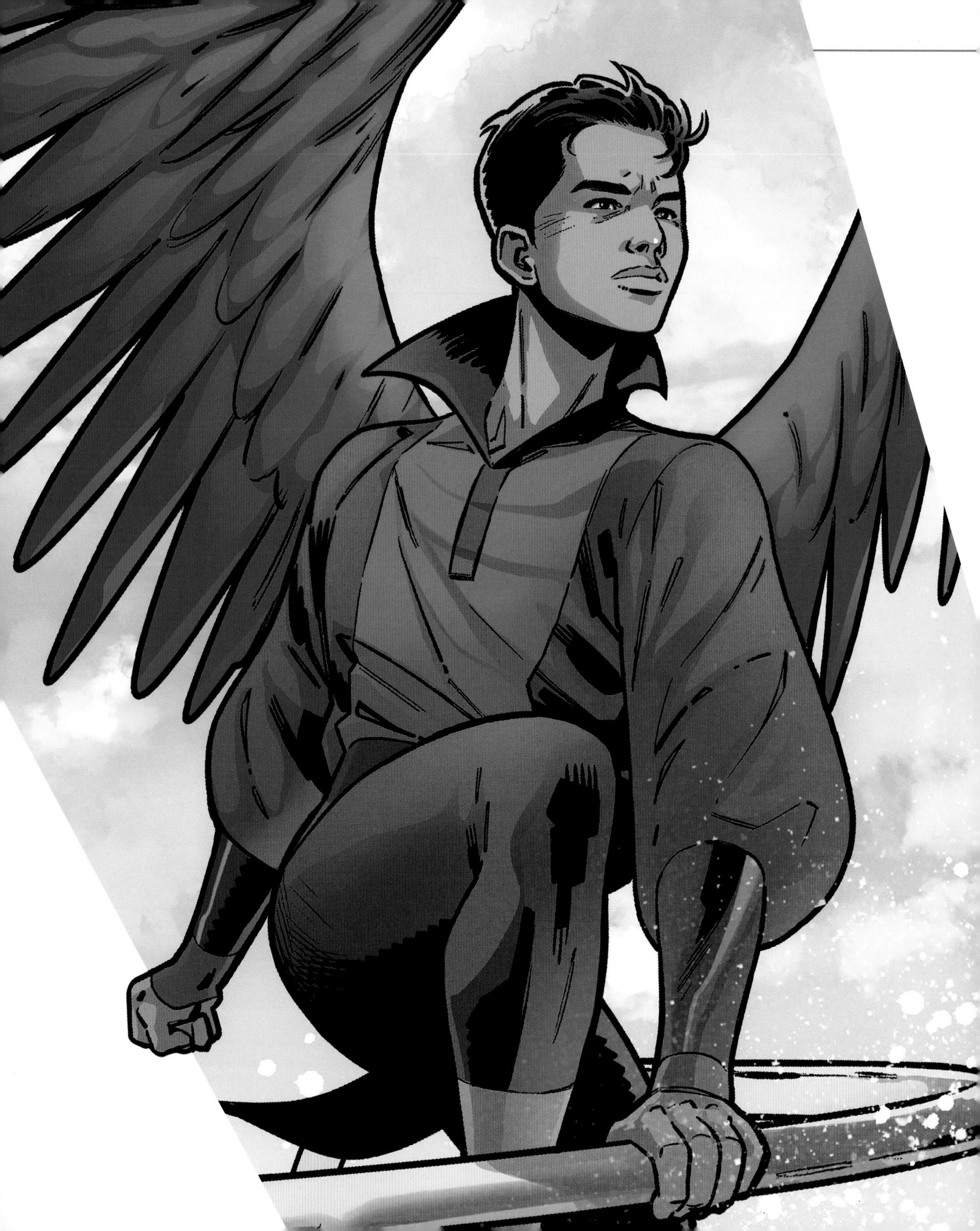

THE AERIE

They/them

"We **sacrificed** a lot to stop this. It's the reason I have **wings.**"

When they were young, the child that would become known as The Aerie was kidnapped in an attempt to coerce their mother, the Badhnisian president. The perpetrators soon realized that the president wouldn't falter, so The Aerie was forced to become a test subject for the Post-Human Project. This nefarious group experimented on The Aerie, giving them wings and the ability to fly. Whilst imprisoned at an island facility, The Aerie met and fell in love with fellow captive Wink. Their bond gave the pair the strength to attempt an escape. During the flight, Wink gave The Aerie their new name.

The Aerie and Wink then joined The Revolutionaries, a team of superpowered individuals fighting for a better world. But on their first mission together, The Aerie and the rest of the Revolutionaries were taken captive by Amanda Waller and forced to join the Suicide Squad. Thankfully, they both managed to survive their experiences on Task Force X, and are now important members of Jay Nakamura's activism group, The Truth.

Through all the hardship and difficulties The Aerie has experienced, they know that as long as they have Wink by their side, there is nothing they cannot rise above.

DATA FILE

First appearance: *Suicide Squad* (Vol. 6) #1 (2020)
Allies: Wink, Jay Nakamura, Superman (Jon Kent), Harley Quinn

Likes: Clear skies, a cool breeze, strawberry ice cream
Dislikes: Hypocrites, light pollution

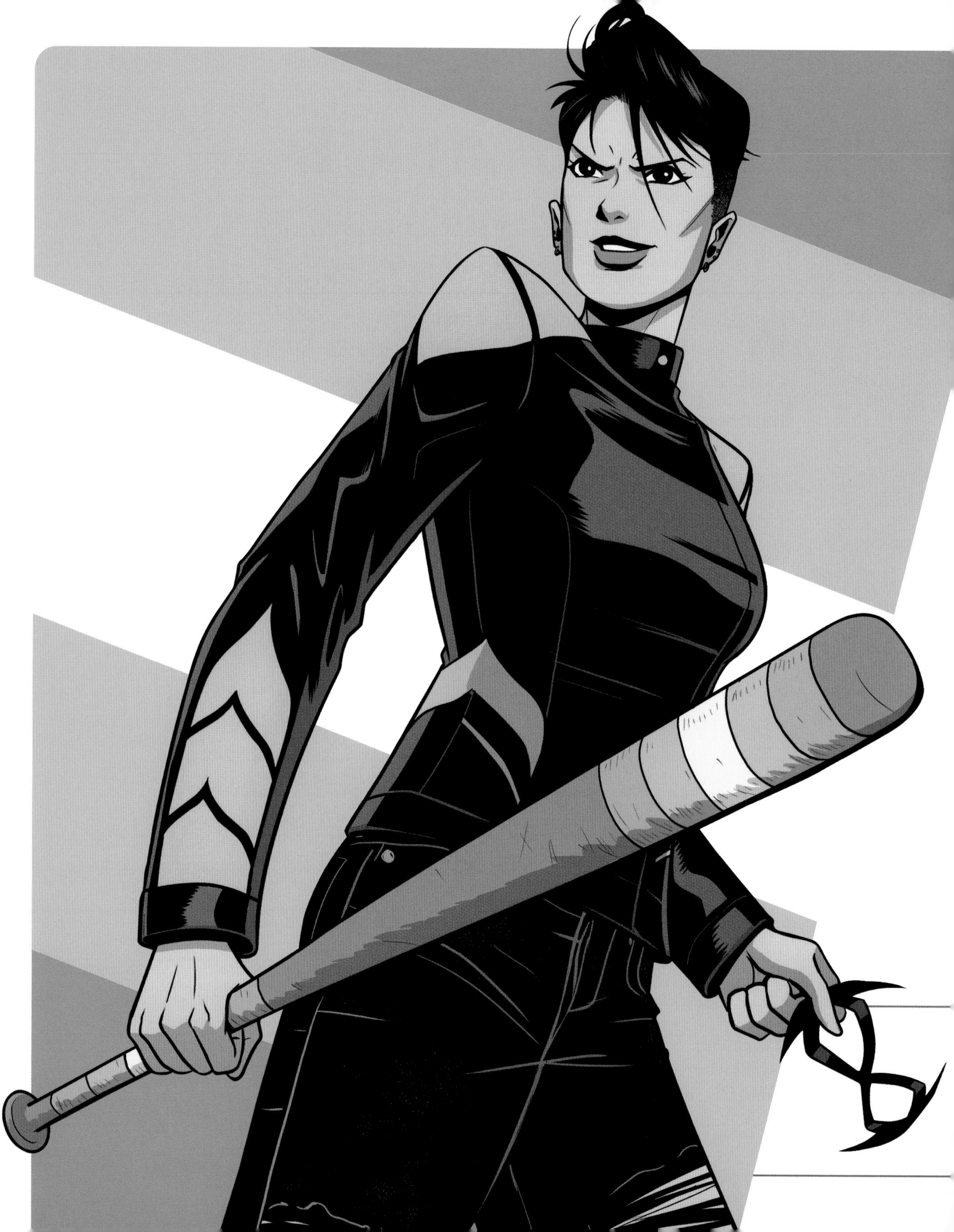

ALYSIA YEOH

She/her

"Please. I'm a **trans woman** in Gotham. Of course I have a **weapon.**"

When Alysia Yeoh, a transgender woman, became Barbara Gordon's roommate, she had no idea she shared a home with the heroic Batgirl. But Alysia is no stranger to danger—as a hardcore activist, she is prepared to put herself in harm's way for what she believes is right. Power-hungry Super-Villains like The Joker are just another group of bullies who need to be stopped at all costs.

For a brief time, Alysia dated Barbara's brother—James Gordon, Jr. However, she later fell in love with fellow activist Jo Muñoz, and during an altercation with the Super-Villain Ragdoll, the two admitted their feelings for each other. They eventually married, with Barbara as the maid of honor at the wedding. It was the happiest day of Alysia's life.

A talented chef, Alysia has built a culinary empire in Gotham City. She finally opened her dream restaurant, the Red Eye Café, and an exciting pop-up named Alysia's Boba Bar and Café. Alysia was looking forward to leaving her wild days behind, but when an injured Batgirl came to her for help, she wasted no time getting in the mix. Perhaps she's destined to keep fighting crime after all!

DATA FILE

First appearance: *Batgirl* (Vol. 4) #1 (2011)
Allies: Batgirl, Coagula, Victoria October

Likes: Protesting, softball, a good bowl of laksa
Dislikes: Oppression, authority figures

APOLLO

He/him

"You, and anyone else in the world, who thinks they've fallen too far, I'll always pull you back into the light."

When Andrew Pulaski was just 13 years old, he was abducted by aliens. After conducting many experiments on Andrew, the aliens were so impressed by the potential of humans that they decided to turn him into a superpowered being.

By the time Andrew managed to flee and return to Earth, he possessed abilities beyond his wildest dreams. Gaining his powers from the sun's energy, Andrew was now able to fly; his body possessed incredible strength; he could shoot lasers out of his eyes; and it was almost impossible for anything to hurt him. Andrew took the name "Apollo" and began working as a vigilante, using his powers to protect people from some of the most corrupt and dangerous organizations around the world.

Apollo was eventually invited to join Stormwatch, an ancient group of Super Heroes striving to protect Earth from alien threats, and soon fell for his teammate Midnighter. Together, they created the Super Hero team The Authority, and their love and devotion for each other has made them one of the world's strongest couples, able to face any challenge.

DATA FILE

First appearance: *Stormwatch* (Vol. 2) #4 (1998)
Allies: Midnighter, Superman (Clark Kent), Steel (Natasha Irons), Extraño

Likes: Hot tea, classic literature, sappy romance novels
Dislikes: How Midnighter keeps stealing the covers

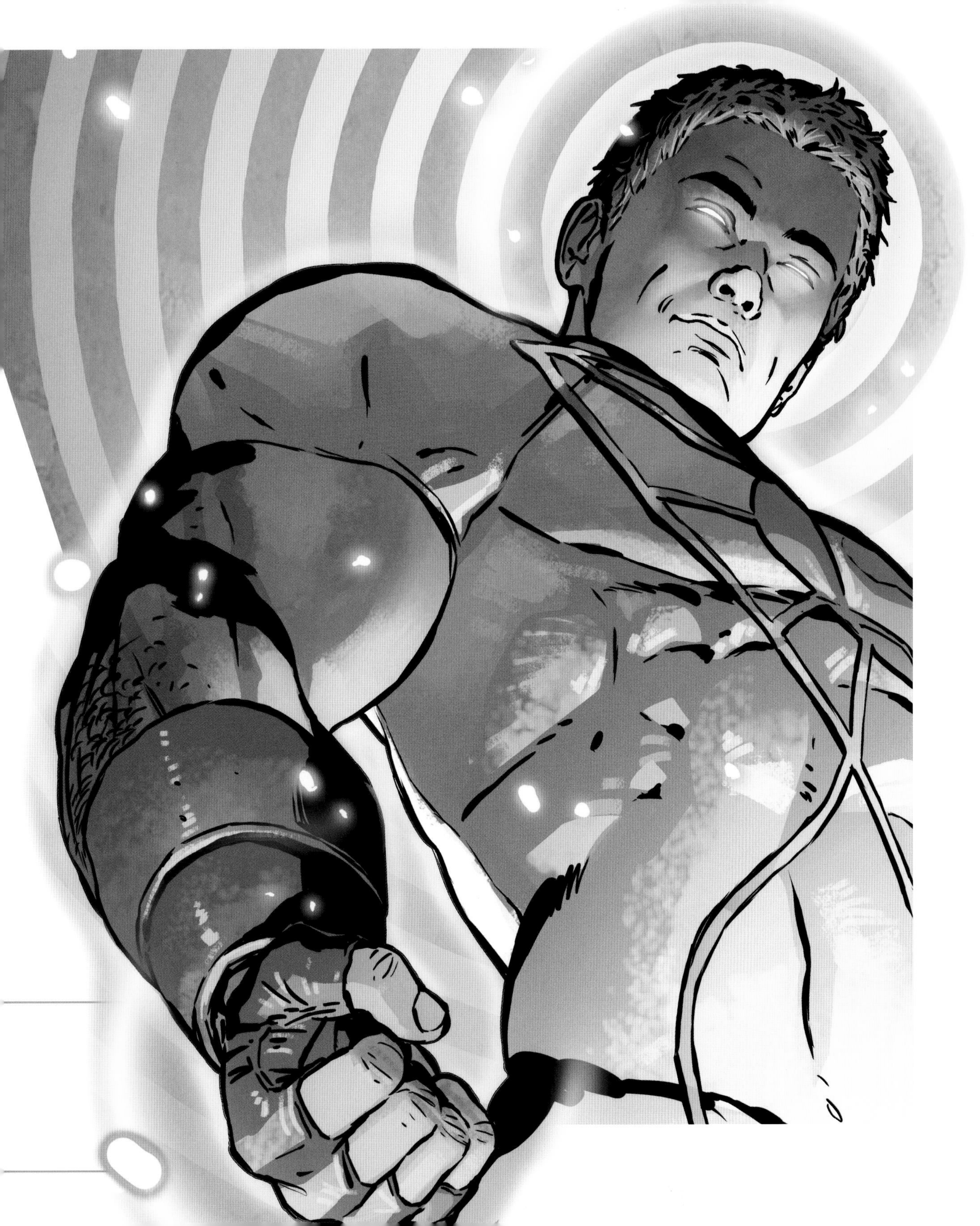

AQUAMAN
(JACKSON HYDE)
He/him

"**Destiny** is a corny word, but it captures what I can't **ignore**: this is where I **belong**."

Jackson Hyde's father is the aquatic Super-Villain Black Manta, and his mother, Lucia Hyde, is a revolutionary from the undersea kingdom of Xebel. Yet Jackson grew up in one of the driest places in the world, a small town in New Mexico where his mother tried to hide them both from his father and her violent past. Jackson developed his water-manipulation powers in secret and rebelled against his mother's desire for him to not stand out by running away to live as his true self.

Jackson's heroic journey began when, after a stunning underwater rescue, he joined the Super Hero team Teen Titans under the name Aqualad. After a short stint on the team, Jackson decided to ask Arthur Curry, the first Aquaman, for training. Arthur agreed and has since shared the title of Aquaman with Jackson, who has proven himself worthy of that legacy time and time again.

Though easily flustered, Jackson has begun a relationship with Ha'Wea, a Xebelian soldier happy to help his desert-raised boyfriend rediscover his aquatic roots.

DATA FILE
First appearance: *DCU: Rebirth* (Vol. 1) #1 (2016)
Allies: Aquaman (Arthur Curry), Mera, Superman (Jon Kent)

Abilities: Gills for underwater breathing, hydrokinesis
Likes: Greasy diner food, slushies, tabletop games
Base: Amnesty Bay

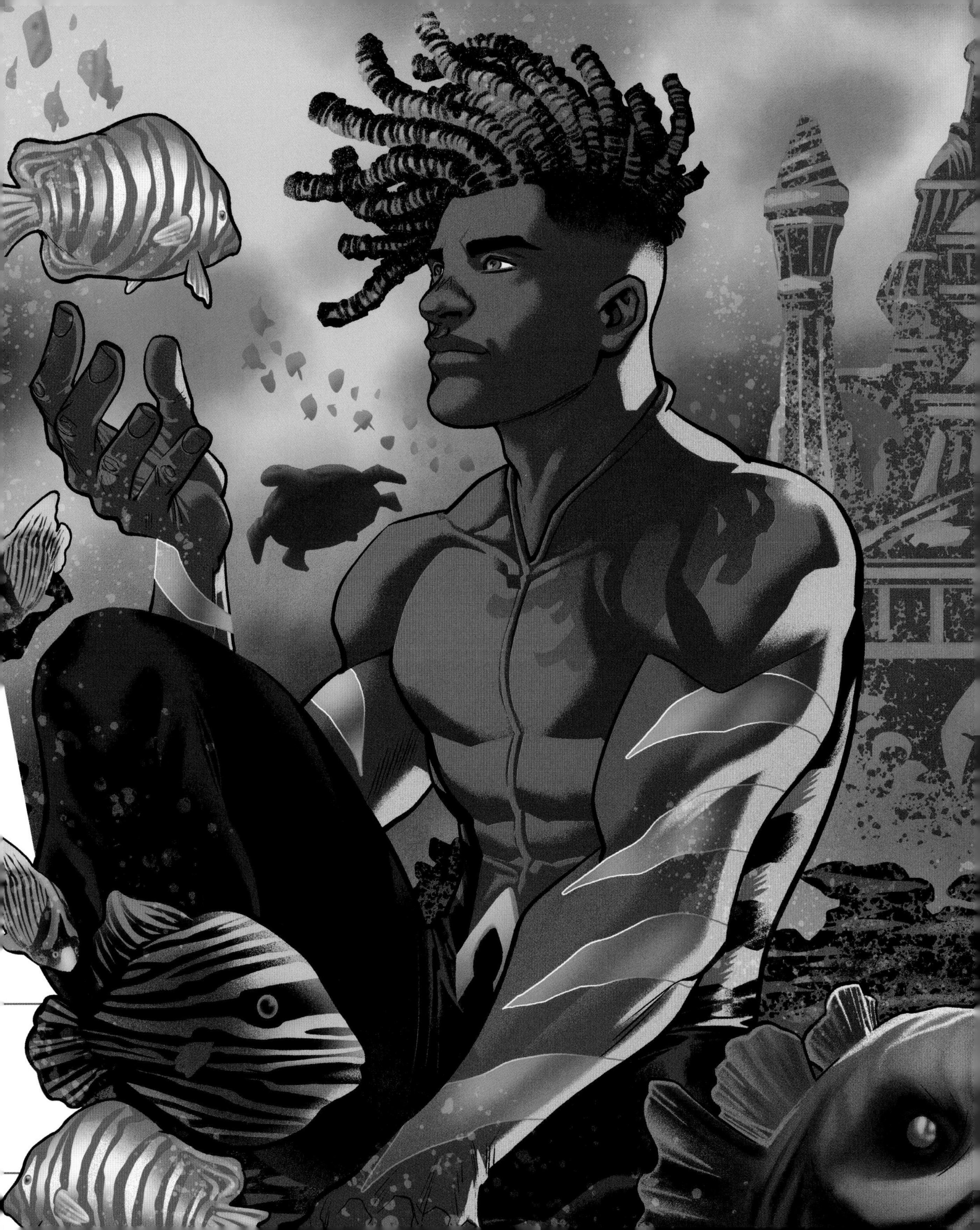

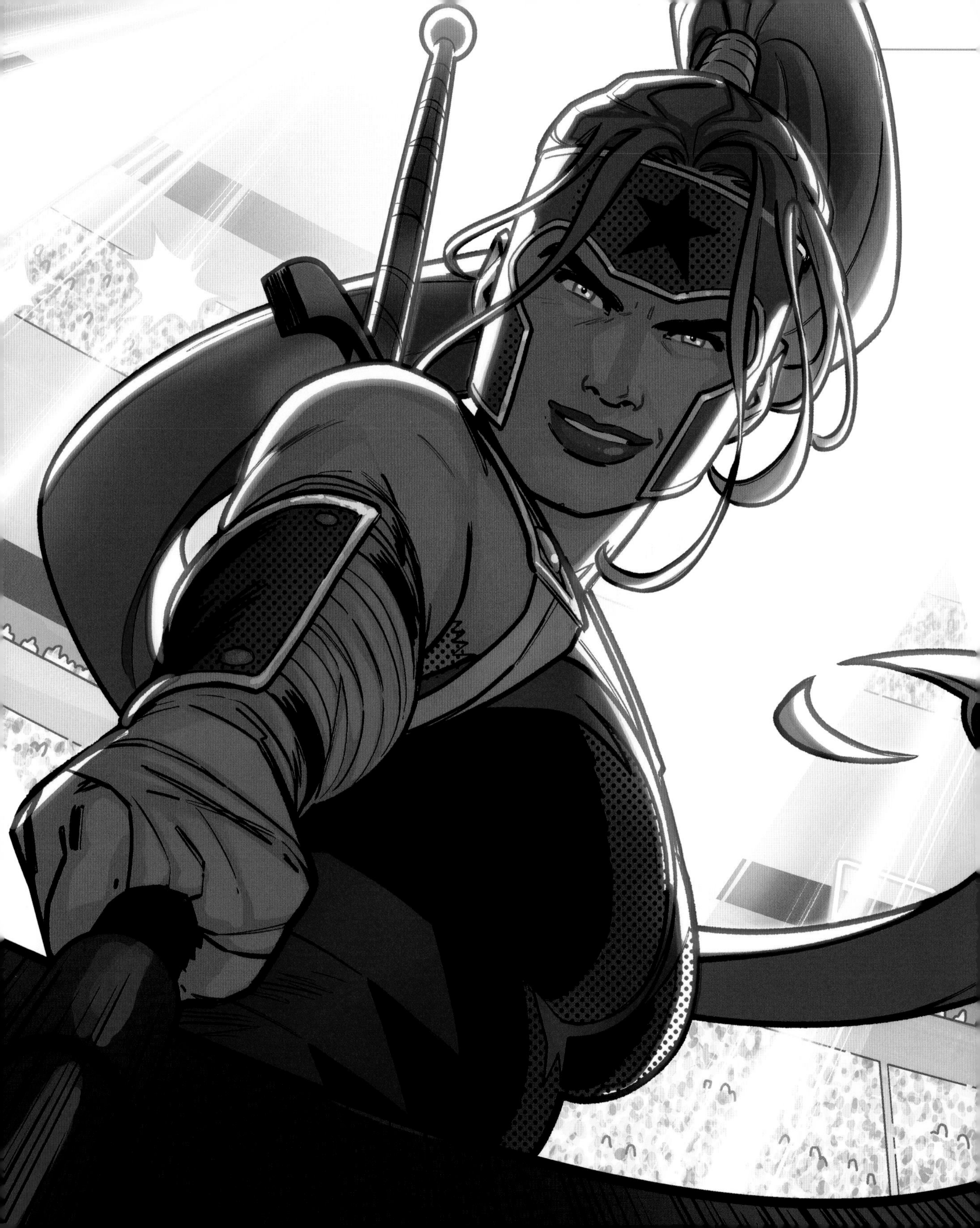

ARTEMIS

She/her

"I have a confession. I didn't need rescuing. I needed a worthy opponent."

Artemis is a fierce warrior, even by Amazonian standards. She is a proud member of the Bana-Mighdall, a group of Amazons who left Themyscira and settled in Egypt. Artemis once challenged Princess Diana for the title of Wonder Woman—and won! Her time as Wonder Woman was short-lived, but she proved that her more warlike methods were highly effective.

Artemis's hotheaded demeanor is second only to her steadfast loyalty to her friends and allies. She served with distinction in the Justice League, was a member of the covert vigilante team the Outlaws and, for a time, led the Bana-Mighdall. A queer woman, Artemis's heart always belonged to her friend Akila. However, Akila was corrupted by the powerful Bow of Ra and caused much destruction. To save the world, Artemis had to kill her—an act Artemis never forgave herself for.

Artemis played a key role in The Trial of the Amazons, when Hippolyta asked Artemis to poison her, kickstarting a series of events that changed the Amazons forever. The warrior will do anything for her sisters and has since been blessed by the new goddess Hippolyta with magic.

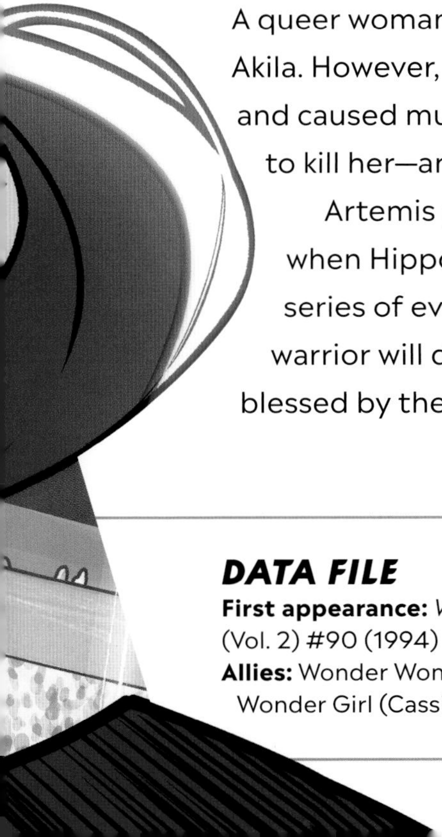

DATA FILE

First appearance: *Wonder Woman* (Vol. 2) #90 (1994)

Allies: Wonder Woman, Queen Faruka II, Wonder Girl (Cassie Sandsmark)

Likes: Swords, axes, bows

Dislikes: Long speeches, jeans

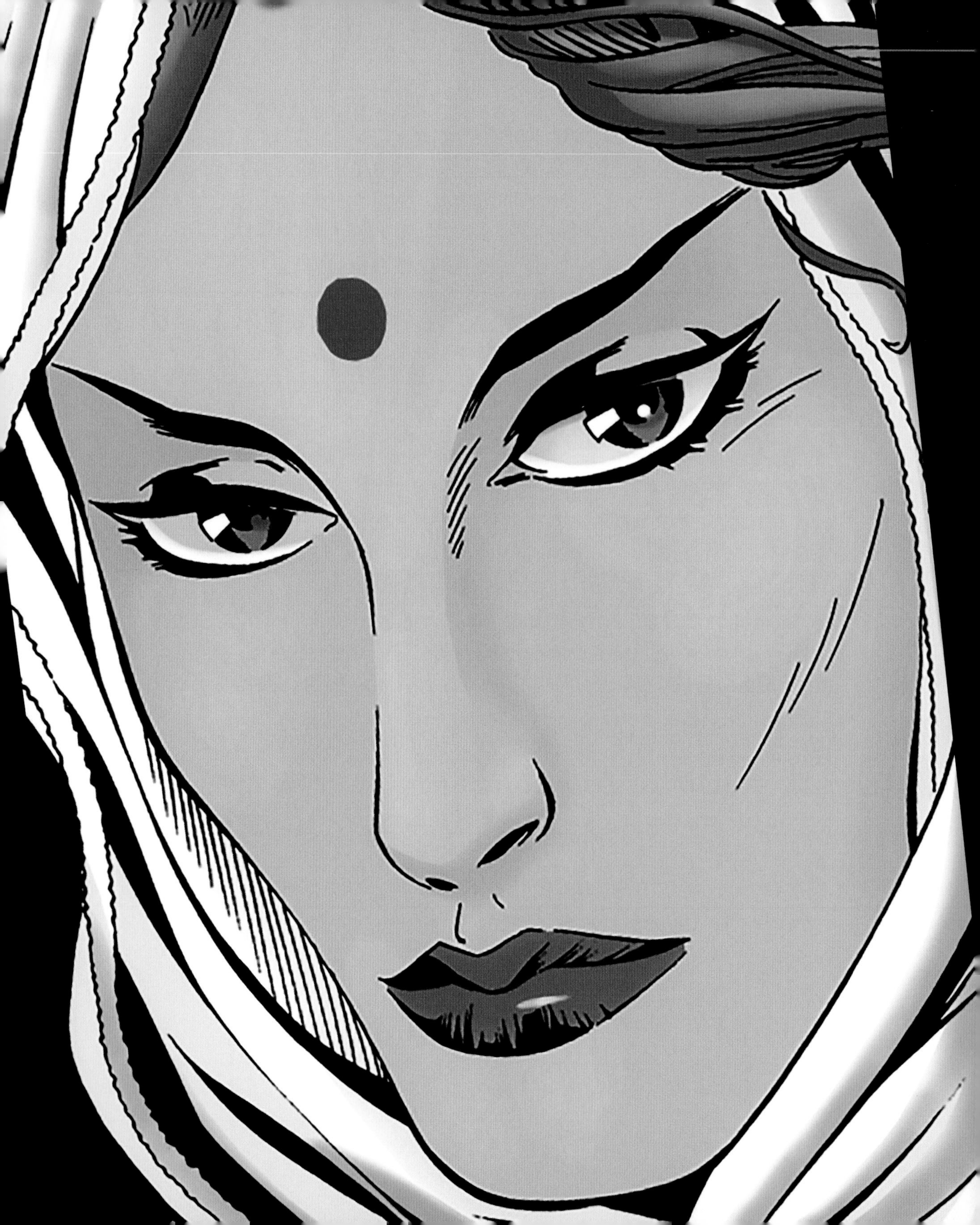

ARUNA SHENDE

Accepts all pronouns

"It is said that a **river** never stops **changing.** Why should I be any **different?**"

Aruna Shende grew up in Chennai, India. They were born with shape-shifting powers that allowed them to mimic the children around them. After Aruna's parents mysteriously disappeared, they wandered from city to city, stealing to survive and working hard to develop control over their powers. At this stage in their life, Aruna's identity was enormously fluid, as they could become male or female, old or young—whatever would make life easier at the time.

It was not until they started working on a movie that Aruna began to grow into the hero they are known as today. Aruna used their powers to become a popular actor and stuntperson in the Indian film industry, convincing their coworkers that their transformations were nothing more than the work of a talented makeup artist. After a chance encounter with Batgirl, Aruna saw that they could be more than just a movie star. They have become an acrobatic champion for justice, using their powers to make a difference in India and fight for those who have been forgotten.

DATA FILE

First appearance: *Batgirl Annual* (Vol. 1) #1 (2000)
Base: Mumbai, India
Occupations: Thief, actor, stuntperson

Likes: Eating sundal, leaping from great heights

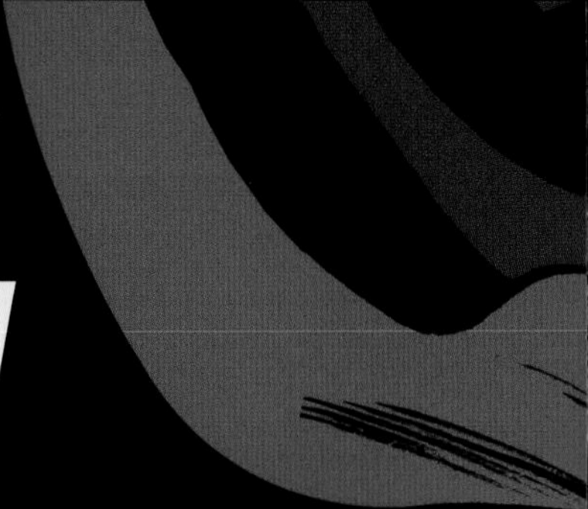

BATWOMAN

(KATE KANE)

She/her

"The truth is that I left as your lost little girl and came back knowing exactly who I am."

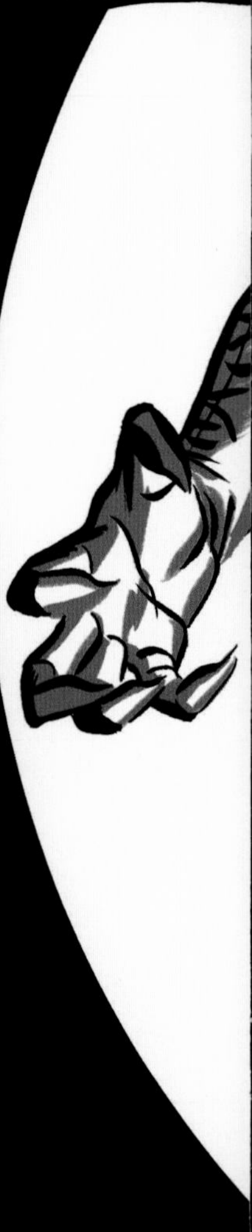

Kate Kane dreamed of graduating from the elite military academy West Point, just like her father did. But that dream was snatched away when, just before her graduation, Kate was met with homophobic prejudice. Kate was told she could avoid being expelled by denying that she was a lesbian. Unashamed of her sexuality and refusing to lie, Kate was forced to leave the academy.

But Kate never lost her desire to serve the public. After a chance encounter with Batman, who is secretly Kate's cousin Bruce Wayne, she realized that she could protect others by becoming a vigilante. Armed with her extensive military training and a vast collection of high-tech gadgetry, Kate was ready to fight crime as Batwoman.

As Kate's skill and renown have grown, she has also taken to teaching the younger members of the Batman Family how to navigate the tough, crime-ridden streets of Gotham City. But while Kate defeats any villain she comes across, she has had much less luck keeping a steady partner. Being a hero and maintaining a

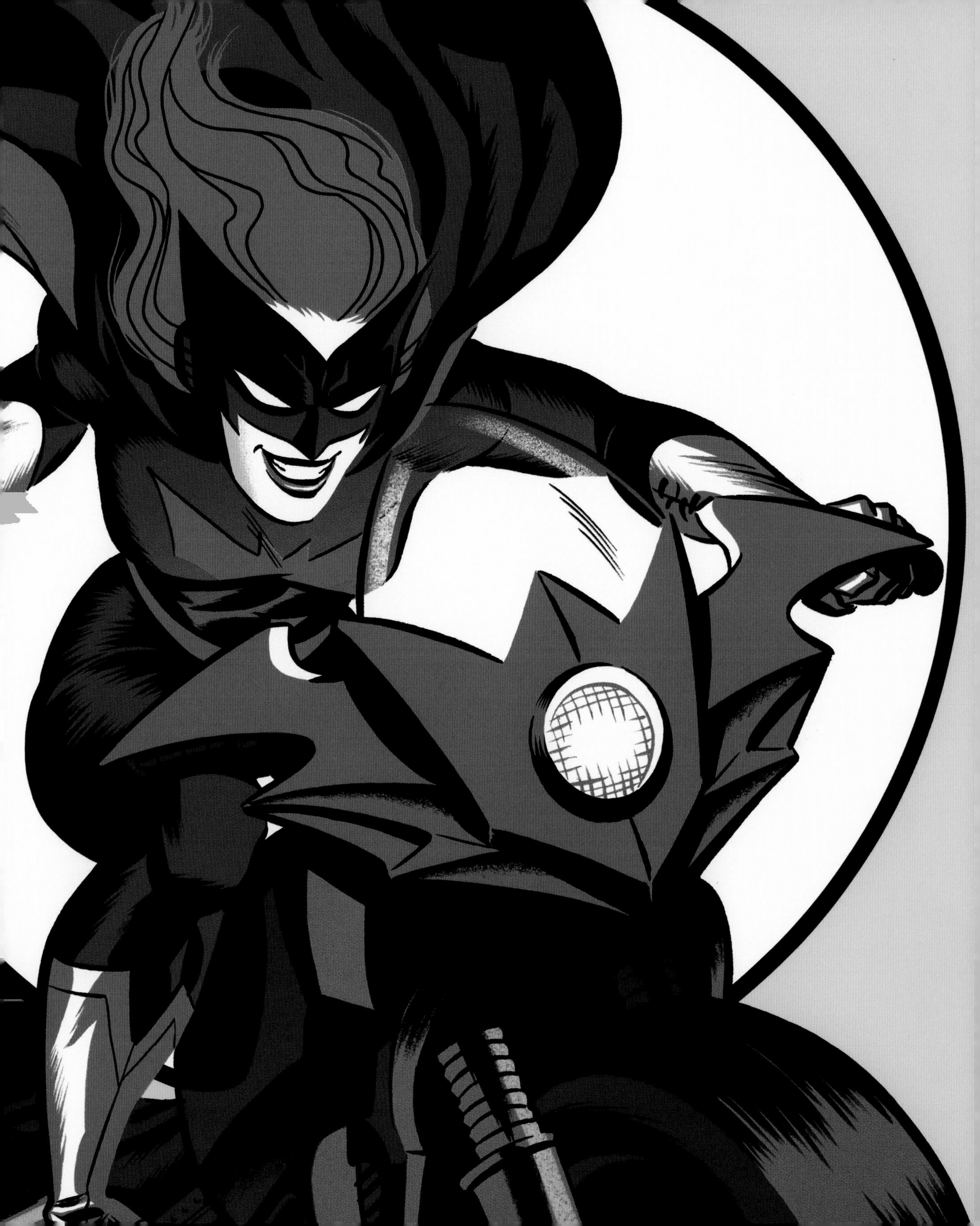

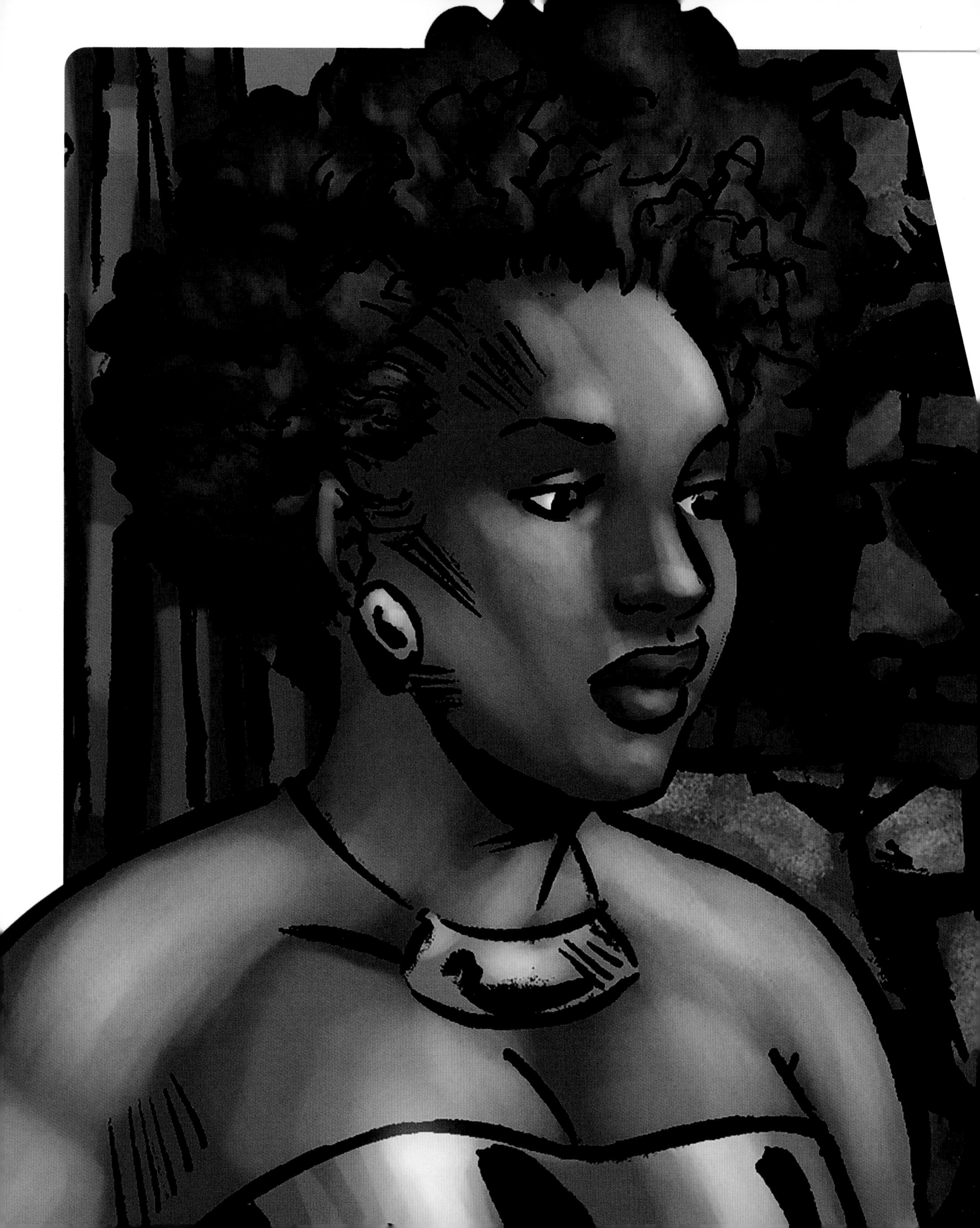

BIA

She/her

"This exact moment feels like my soul has desired it long before I came here. I am Bia!"

The past of Bia, a trans Amazon, is a mystery. Her history is shrouded, even to herself, as her emergence from the Well of Souls on Themyscira left her without any memories of her previous life. Who she was on Earth before her death and then rebirth as an Amazon remains to be revealed.

If Bia ever found it hard losing her memories, she never showed it. She quickly became part of Amazonian society, impressing the warriors with her wisdom and intelligence. Bia has exhibited the gift of precognition—seeing events before they happen. This ability, along with her kindness and deep insight into human nature, led to her becoming one of Queen Nubia's most trusted advisors.

Perhaps this is why Bia seems happy to forget her past. Now that she has found a home where she can truly belong, the one she left behind could not possibly compare.

DATA FILE

First appearance: *Nubia and the Amazons* (Vol. 1) #1 (2021)
Allies: Nubia, Io, Philippus

Likes: Hearty breakfasts, bangles
Dislikes: Overly complicated sandals

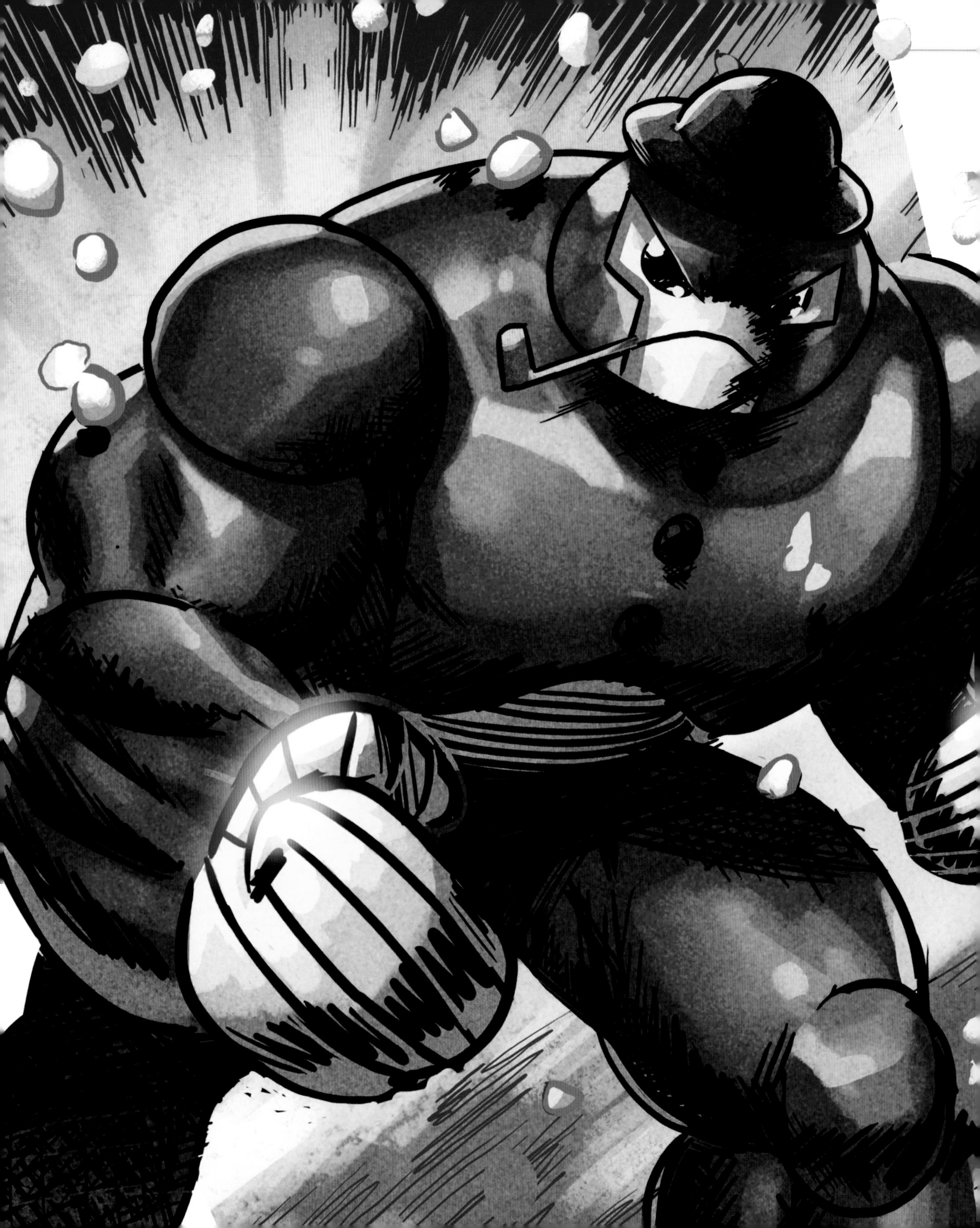

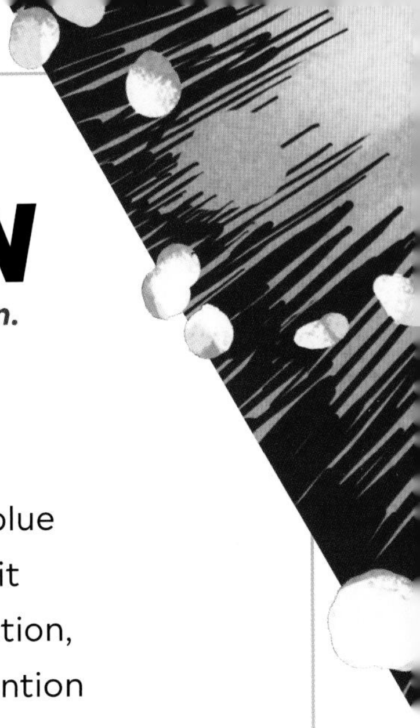

BLUE SNOWMAN

Byrna is still working out the whole pronouns situation.

"An unconscious Amazon can't resist blue snow! Ha! Haaaa!"

Byrna Brilyant's father was the inventor of hyper-cold blue snow that never melted and instantly froze whatever it touched. He died before getting the chance to see it in action, but Byrna decided to continue his work and used this invention to become the Super-Villain Blue Snowman.

Byrna crafted several robots, and with their help used blue snow to threaten a group of innocent farmers' crops. After being defeated by Wonder Woman, the Blue Snowman attempted to get revenge as part of Super-Villain team Villainy Inc.

While under the influence of Wonder Woman's Lasso of Truth, Brilyant revealed that Blue Snowman had felt like the right name, because sometimes Byrna felt like a man and at other times a woman. It was during this encounter that Blue Snowman learned about the term *genderfluid*. Discovering there was a word for this identity gave Byrna lots to think about, and Wonder Woman hoped that this would bring the villain some peace.

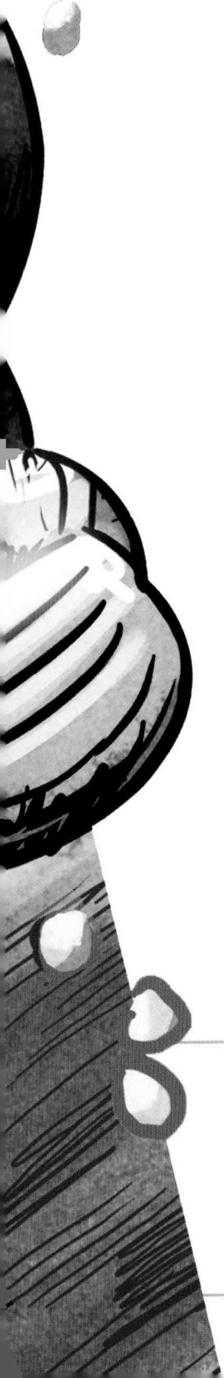

DATA FILE

First appearance: *Sensation Comics* (Vol. 1) #59 (1946)
Base: Fair Weather Valley
Occupation: Robotics engineer
Likes: Money, the color blue, bowler hats

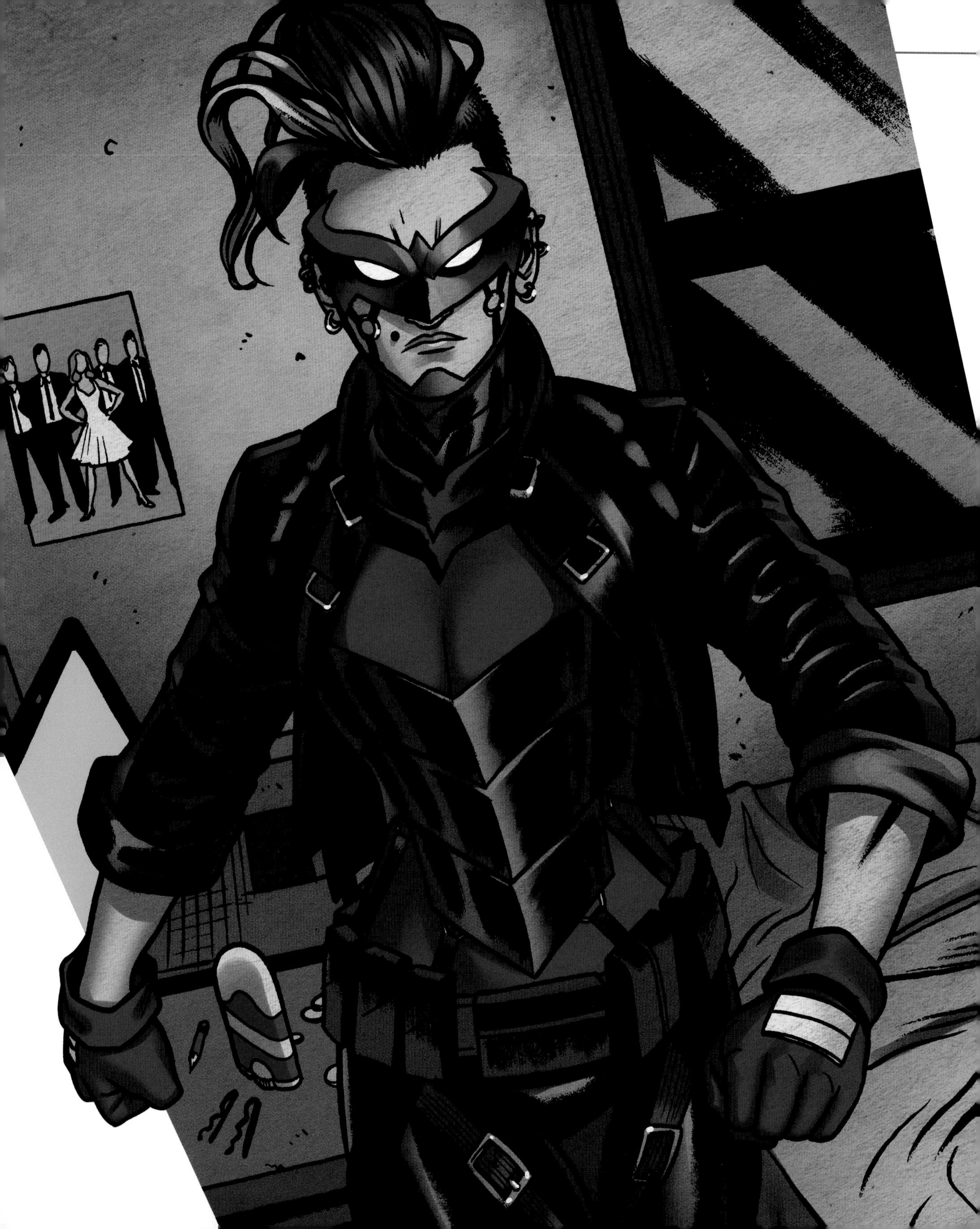

BLUEBIRD

She/her

"Just your friendly neighborhood... uh... taser girl."

Bisexual electronics genius Harper Row just wanted to protect her younger brother, Cullen. Using her homemade tasers, Harper attempted to save him from a gang of homophobic bullies, but there were too many people for her to fight alone. Fortunately, Batman saved Harper and Cullen.

Harper worked tirelessly to repay Batman, helping him several times and eventually becoming the vigilante Bluebird. Armed with gadgets of her own design—including impact armor, electromagnetic pulse generators, and a variety of other devices that fire electricity—Bluebird became an important member of the Batman Family. Among many adventures, Bluebird has defeated the Super-Villains Mad Hatter and Mother and defended others the way she looks after Cullen.

Harper has since focused on completing her college education. But she keeps all her gadgets and gear, and recently suited up once again to face the villain Punchline. Perhaps Gotham City needs Bluebird more than Harper thinks.

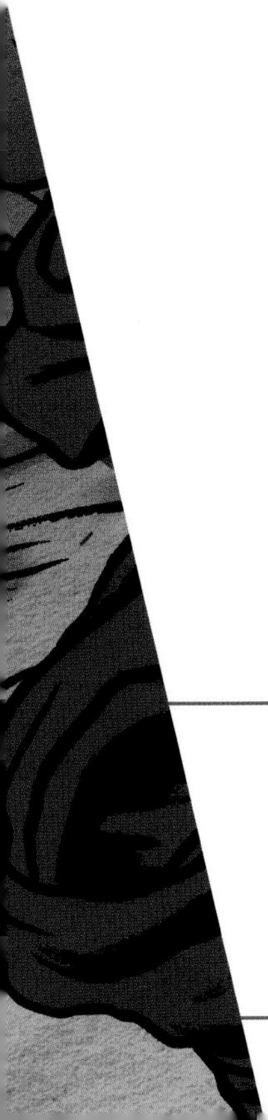

DATA FILE

First appearance: *Batman* (Vol. 2) #1 (2012)
Allies: Batman, Batwoman (Kate Kane), Catwoman, Robin (Tim Drake), Batgirl (Stephanie Brown), Batgirl (Cassandra Cain)
Likes: Hair dye, new gadgets, looking good in a tuxedo
Dislikes: Rich people

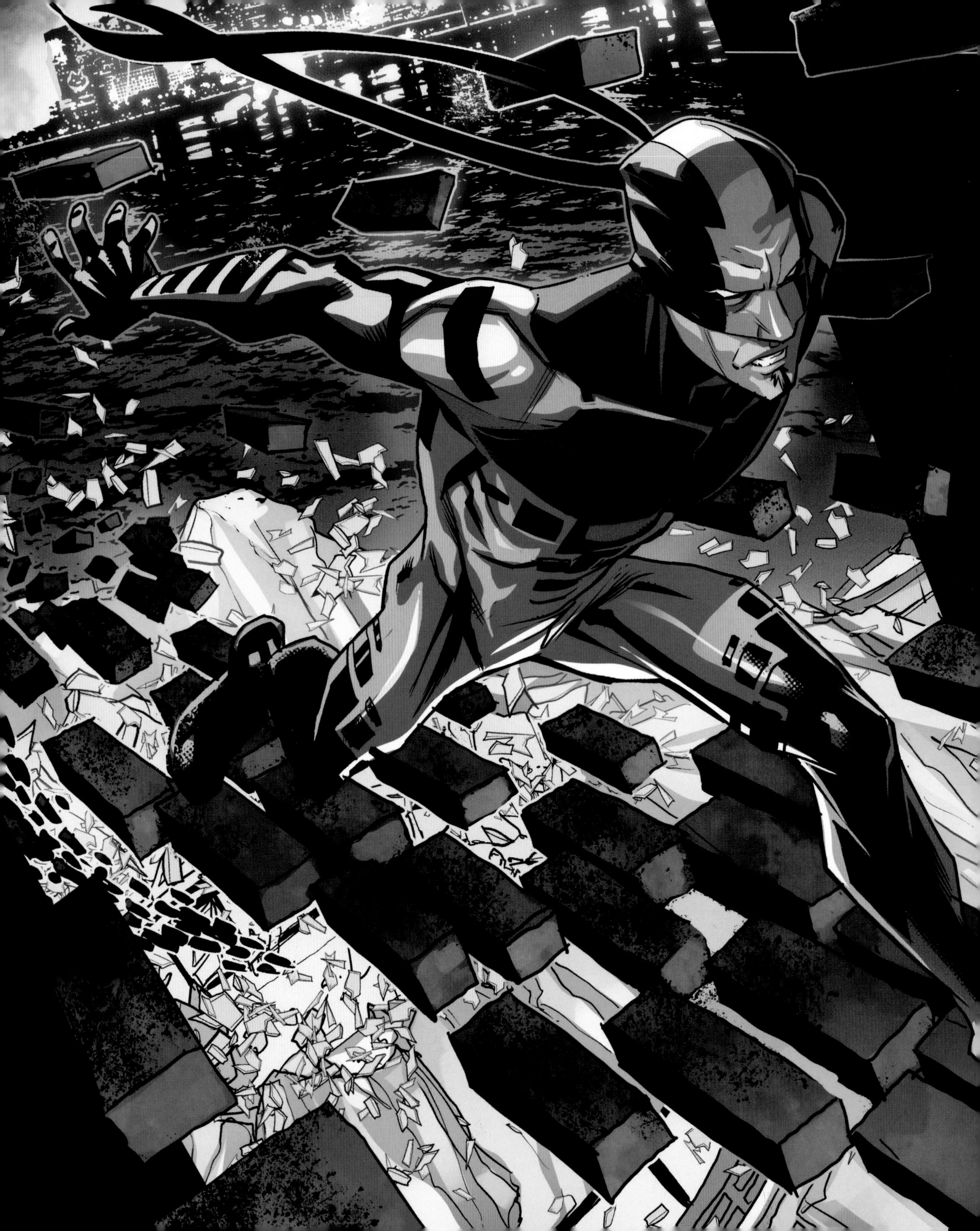

BUNKER

He/him

"I always knew I was different, even before I got metahuman powers. I never tried to hide that fact—not once!"

Out-and-proud gay teenager Miguel Barragan was never going to live in the shadows. Miguel possesses the ability to create glowing "bricks" of psionic energy and uses them to build walls, shields, or even giant fists, instantly drawing a crowd. And if his sparkling superpower doesn't grab people's attention, his boisterous, witty personality will!

Although Miguel enjoyed life in his hometown El Chilar in Mexico, he decided to leave so that he could put his powers to good use. After becoming the Super Hero Bunker, he soon joined the Teen Titans, gaining a reputation for being one of the most friendly and optimistic team members. For Miguel, every day as a Super Hero is filled with adventure and excitement.

After being kidnapped and imprisoned by the Super-Villain Solitary, he joined the antihero team known as the Outlaws, carrying out a darker form of justice. But being an antihero didn't suit Miguel, and he eventually came back into the light to train a new generation of Super Heroes at Teen Titans Academy.

DATA FILE

First appearance: *Teen Titans* (Vol. 4) #1 (2011)
Allies: Stitch, Traci 13, Red Arrow, Kid Flash

Likes: Barbacoa, anything purple
Dislikes: Professor Beast Boy's "jokes"

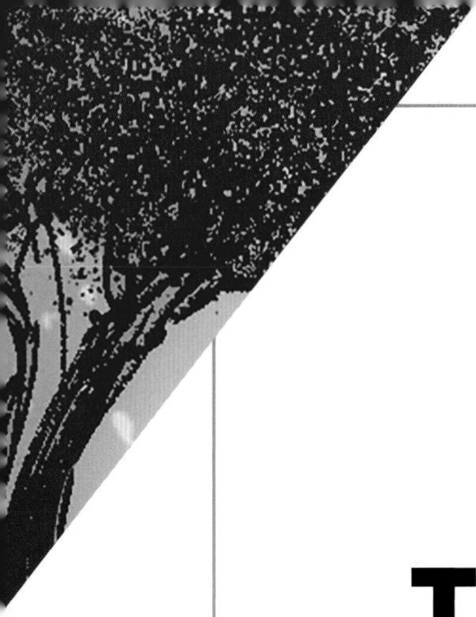

CATMAN

He/him

**"You'll run. You'll hide.
And in the dark, I will find you."**

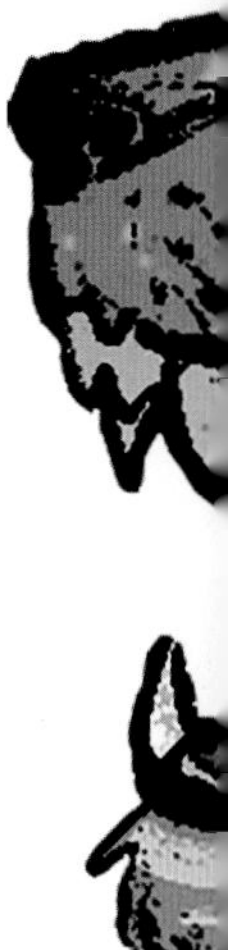

There was a time when Thomas Blake was the greatest hunter the world had ever seen. He was so skilled that capturing lions was too easy for him, which led to him becoming bored with hunting. Thomas decided to turn to a life of crime, hoping that his new identity as Catman would provide the thrills he had lost.

However, Thomas was not a capable criminal. His time as a villain was filled with failure after failure, unsuccessfully contending with both Batman and Catwoman, and he eventually returned to hunting in an attempt to find some peace. To Thomas's surprise, a lion pack welcomed him as one of their own.

After years of living with the pride, Thomas's past as a Super-Villain came back to haunt him, forcing him to put on the cape and cowl of Catman once again. Now neither a hero nor a villain, and with skills from his time with the lions, the agile Catman is a force to be reckoned with and a key member of the mercenary team the Secret Six. Thomas enjoys entertaining the affections of men and women, living his nine lives to the fullest.

DATA FILE

First appearance: *Detective Comics* (Vol. 1) #311 (1963)
Allies: Porcelain, Cheshire, Deadshot, Scandal Savage
Abilities: Tracking, acrobatics, hand-to-hand combat
Likes: Cats, raw meat, knives

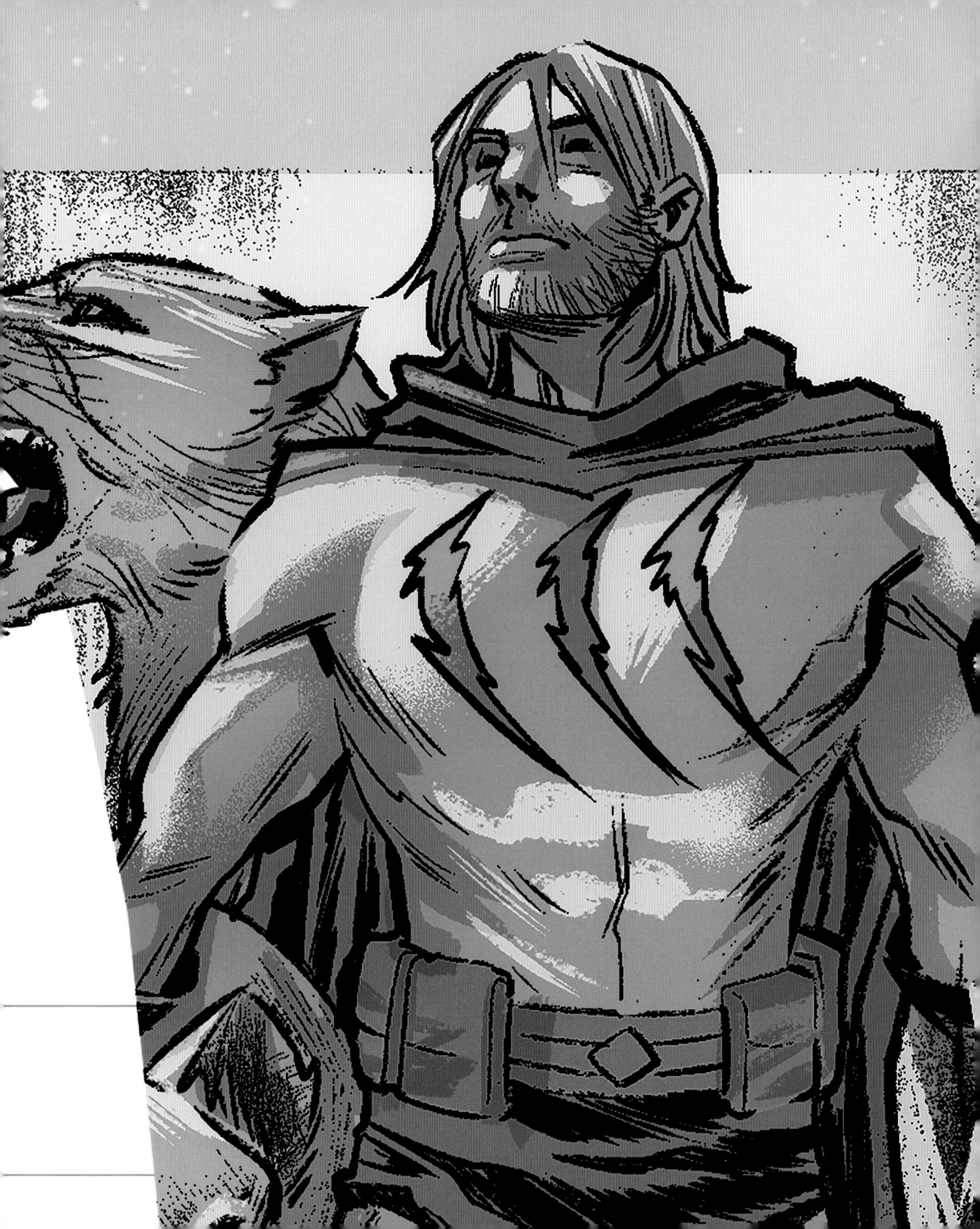

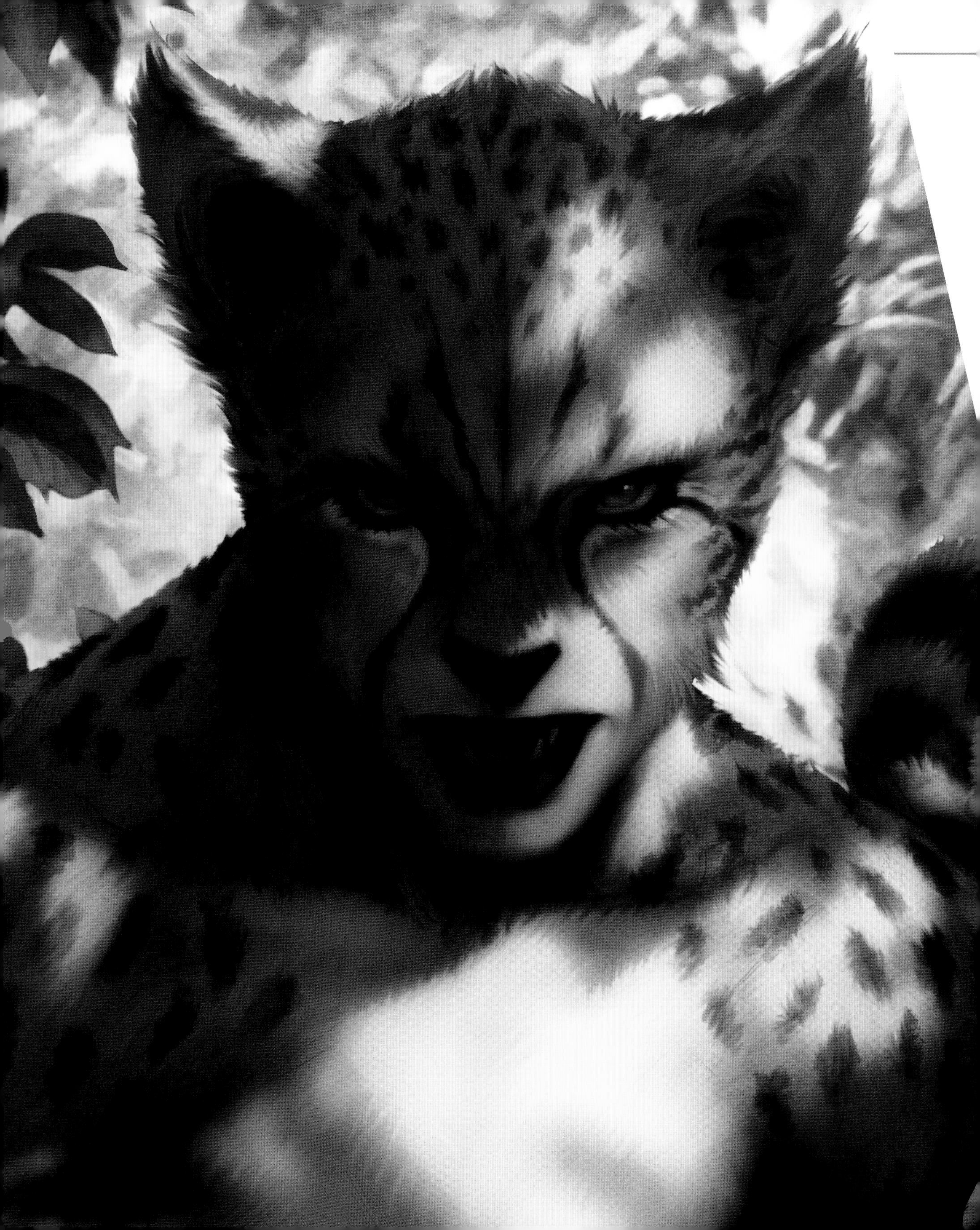

THE CHEETAH
(BARBARA MINERVA)
She/her

"Not everyone can be saved.
Not everyone wants to be saved."

Barbara Minerva always wanted to discover something amazing. She spent years of her archaeological career trying to find evidence of the mythical Amazons, a group she had idolized since childhood. Just when Barbara had almost given up, Lieutenant Etta Candy introduced her to Wonder Woman—living proof of Barbara's dreams. Barbara could translate Diana's language and soon befriended the Amazon, helping her settle away from Themyscira. She also began a relationship with Etta.

Barbara's quest for knowledge would ultimately be her downfall. She traveled to Bwunda in Africa to investigate the plant god Urzkartaga—only to be captured by him. By the time Diana saw Barbara again, Barbara had been transformed into the animalistic Cheetah, complete with superhuman speed and razor-sharp claws. The woman who had been one of Wonder Woman's closest friends was now one of her greatest enemies.

Wonder Woman and Etta tried many times to bring Barbara back to her old self, but there is a part of Barbara that enjoys being the powerful Cheetah. Because of that, she can never fully return to the women who love her.

DATA FILE

First appearance: *Wonder Woman* (Vol. 2) #7 (1987)
Abilities: Enhanced sense of smell, superhuman strength

Likes: Old books
Dislikes: Dogs, people who don't use bookmarks

CIRCUIT BREAKER

He/him/they/them

"Slow down. As they say—measure twice, only risk the destruction of your town once."

Julian "Jules" Jourdain is a transgender man from a Basque rancher family who grew up in a desert town off US Highway 50—"The Loneliest Road in America." Though his parents supported his transition, Jules has been estranged from them since they worked with a company that bought up local land to store thermonuclear waste.

Jules loved giving tours at his hometown's Historical Reenactment Society, which spotlighted the town's claim to fame: when Super-Villain The Turtle brought locals to a standstill with his Still Force powers, and The Flash (Barry Allen) sped through to save the day. But everything changed when Lazarus Rain raged across Earth, granting new superpowers to some and changing the existing abilities of others. Jules suddenly found himself with a connection to what his town most feared: the dreaded Still Force.

Jules proved himself a hero that day, as the same power that The Turtle once used to take over his town enabled him to save it from destruction. Emboldened by his new abilities, Jules took the heroic name Circuit Breaker and vowed to protect his home and the world beyond with an eye toward environmental justice.

DATA FILE

First appearance: *Lazarus Planet: Dark Fate* #1 (2023)
Abilities: Connection to the Still Force allows Jules to decelerate or negate motion and absorb kinetic energy
Likes: Dinosaurs, sequins
Dislikes: Comets, pollution

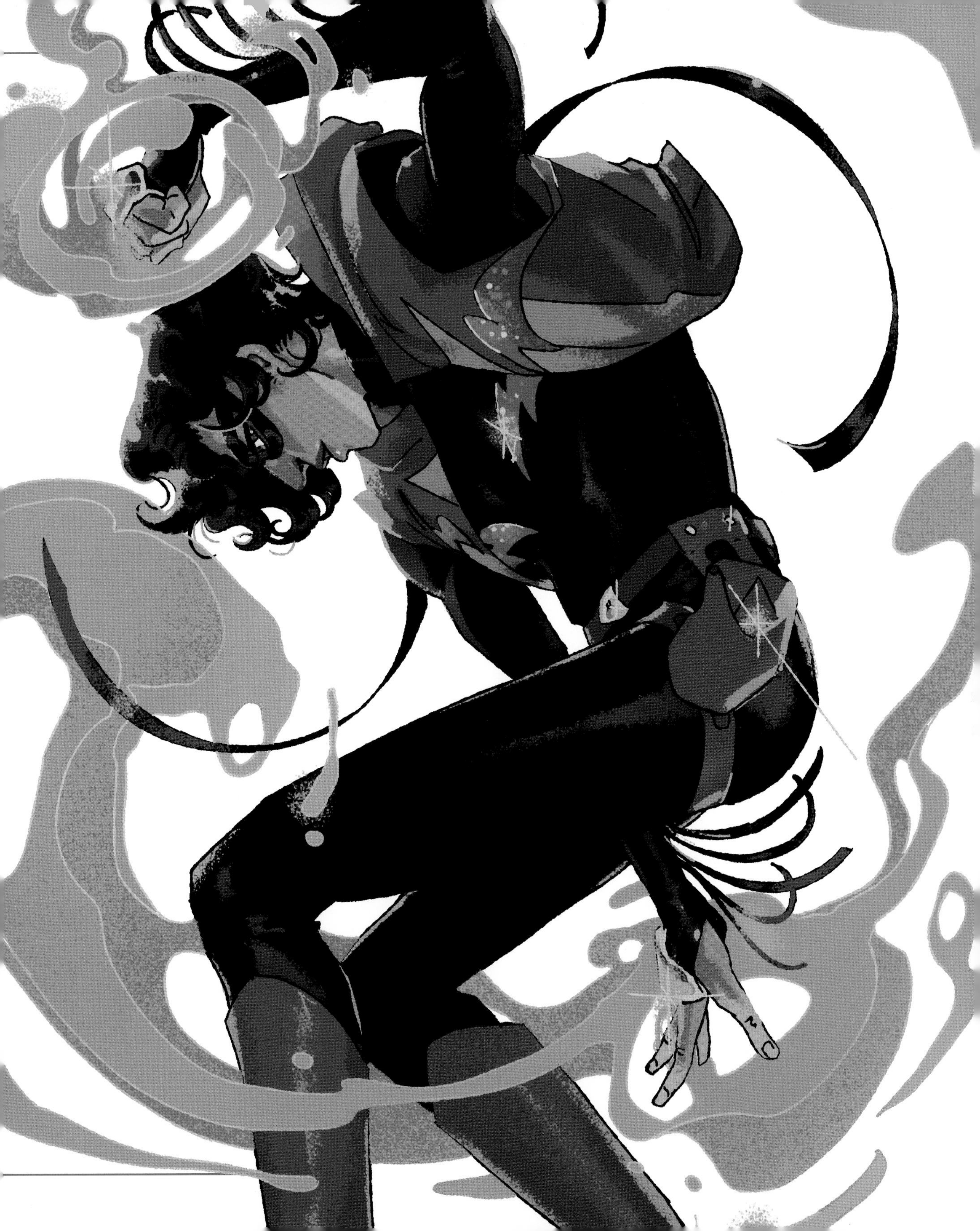

COAGULA

She/her

"I guess I'll just give up the Super Hero business and go on **being myself.**"

Kate Godwin was never looking to save the world—she was just an ordinary transgender woman trying to live her life. However, after an encounter with the Super Hero Rebis, she found herself gifted with the ability to turn solids into liquids and liquids into solids. Not sure what else to do with her new powers, Kate attempted to join the Justice League. While they were impressed with her abilities, they ultimately decided not to admit her to their ranks.

Following this rejection, Kate had abandoned thoughts of becoming a Super Hero, but after stopping the Super-Villain Codpiece, she was invited to join the Doom Patrol and named herself Coagula. Before long, she was protecting the planet from threats that even the Justice League would have trouble dealing with, including single-handedly stopping the godlike beings the Teiresiae from destroying the Earth.

But while Kate found success as a Super Hero, her warmth and wisdom truly made her an essential member of the team. In Kate's eyes, the well-being of her friends and teammates always comes before saving the world.

DATA FILE

First appearance: *Doom Patrol* (Vol. 2) #70 (1993)
Allies: Alysia Yeoh, Rebis, Robotman, Dorothy Spinner

Abilities: Liquid coagulation, dissolving solids
Dislikes: Judgmental people

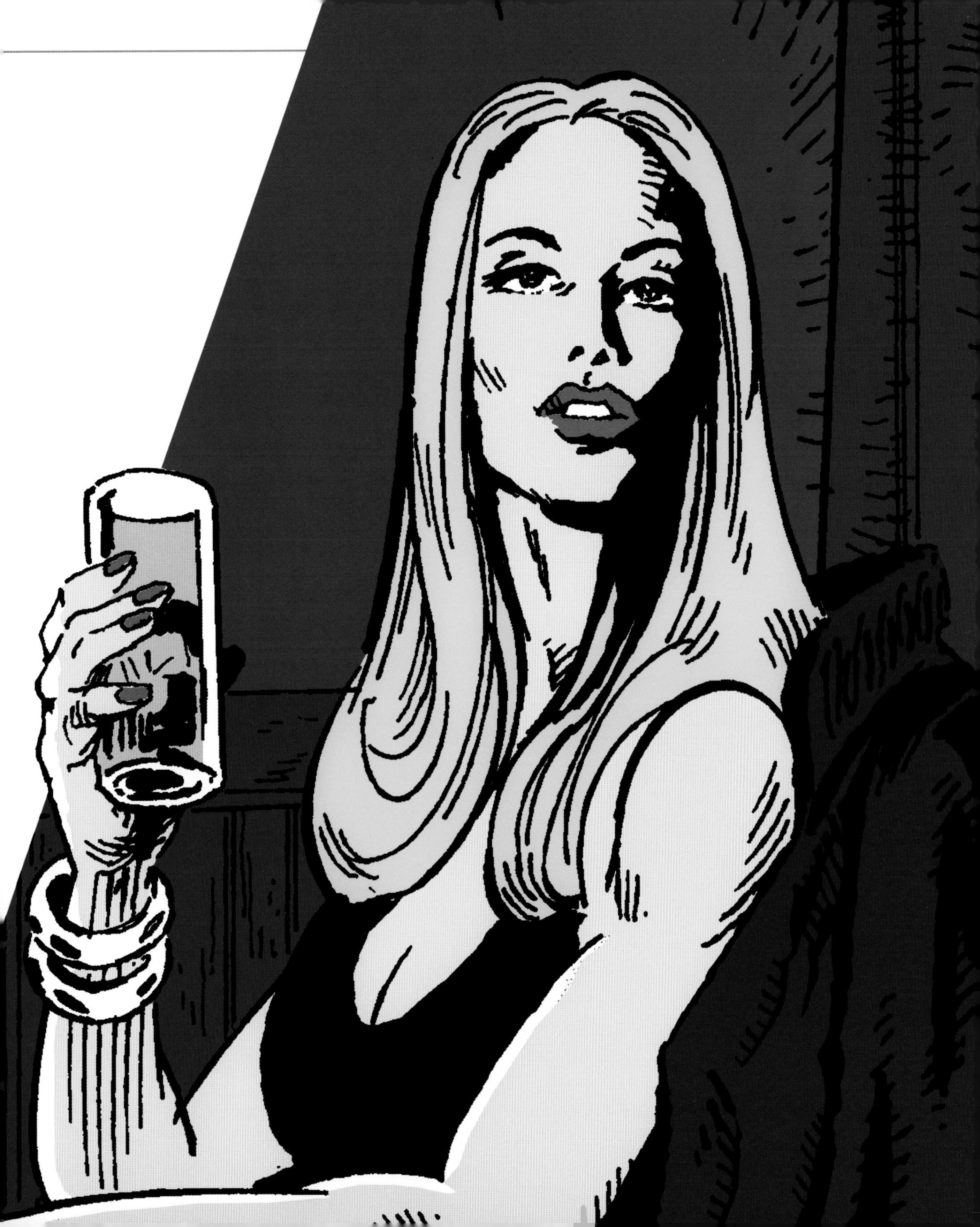

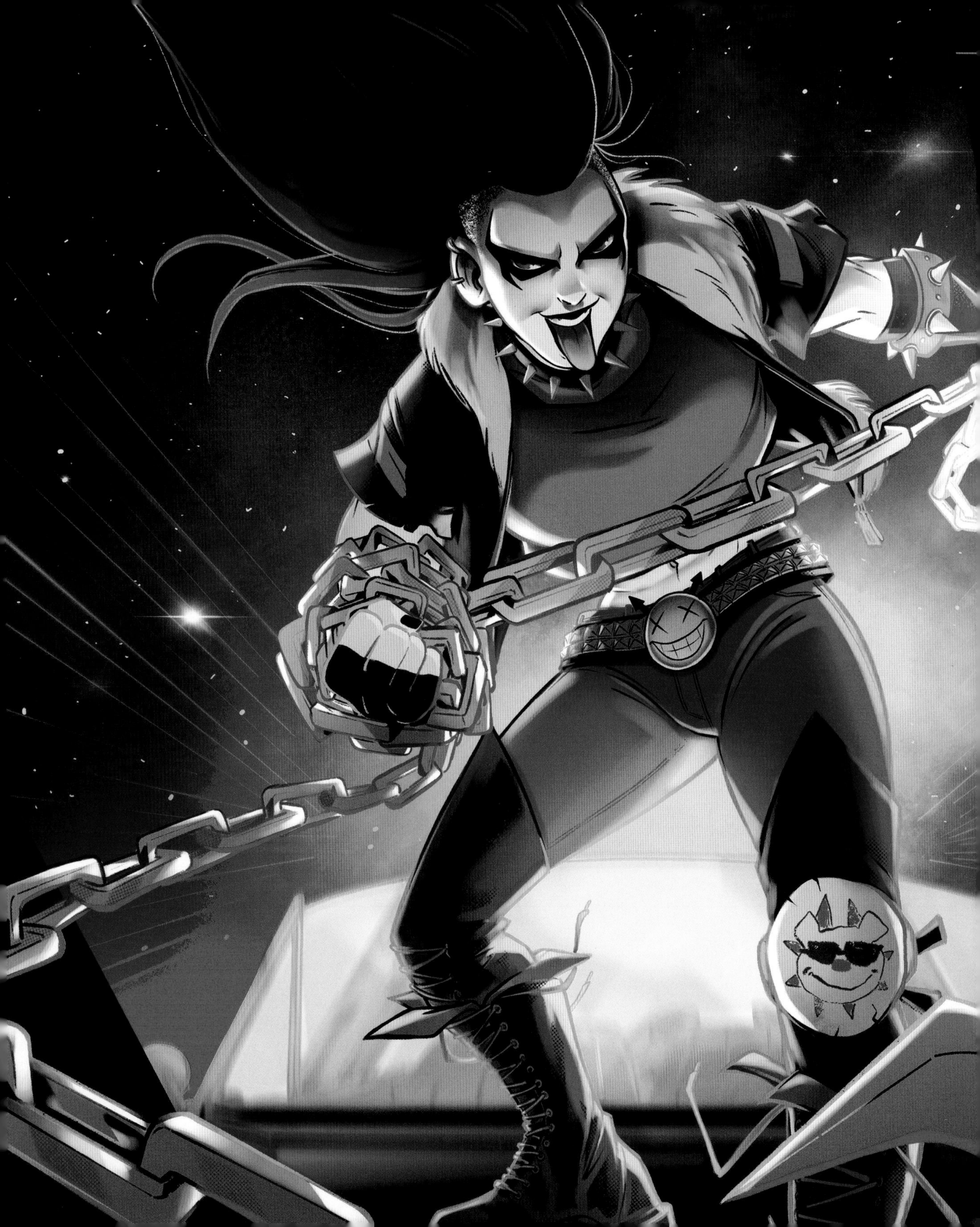

CRUSH

She/her

"I go by Crush, 'cuz that's what I do. Sometimes that gets me in trouble. But I like trouble."

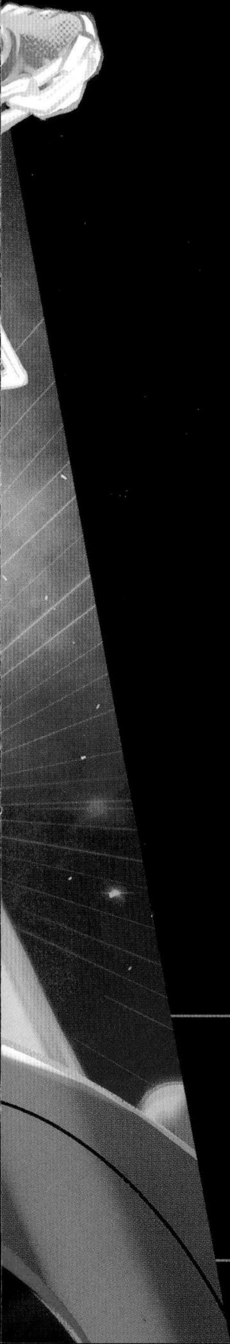

When Crush was just a baby, she crash-landed on Earth, in the United States, during the Burning Man festival. The alien child was adopted by a couple of kindly hippie burnouts at the event, who gave her the name Xiomara Rojas. They told her that her birth parents were Super Heroes from outer space, even though they suspected her birth father was the infamous Super-Villain Lobo due to the family resemblance.

As a teenager, Xiomara got mixed up with an underground alien fight club, taking the name Crush. As word of her fighting abilities spread, Crush was invited to join the Teen Titans. Crush brought her own brand of brash and daring cockiness to the Super Hero team. She helped defeat the Super-Villain Brother Blood and started a short-lived relationship with fellow Titan Djinn. Crush also had her first—but far from last—confrontation with her murderous father, Lobo.

Crush's heart currently belongs to Katie, who she met at a fast-food restaurant's playground. Unlike Crush, Katie is sweet and bubbly, but the two women have fallen hard for each other—proving that opposites really do attract!

DATA FILE

First appearance: *Teen Titans Special* (Vol. 1) #1 (2018)
Allies: Red Arrow, Roundhouse, Kid Flash, Robin (Damian Wayne)
Likes: Sextuple-decker cheeseburgers, travel coffee mugs
Dislikes: Her dad, parallel parking space ships

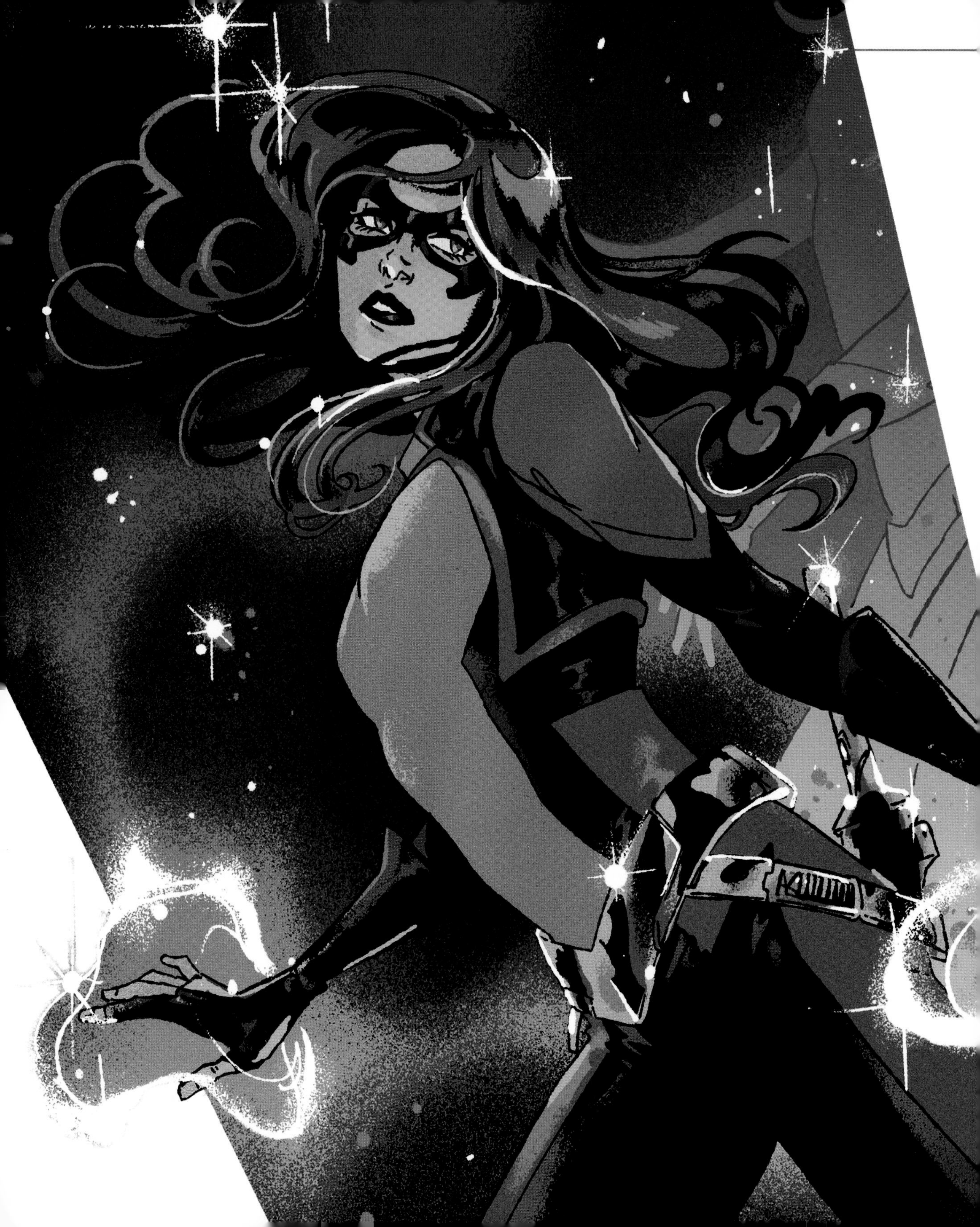

DREAMER

She/her

"If you hurry, you can bust a bank robbery that's about to be in progress. I saw it during my afternoon nap."

Nia Nal comes from a long line of superpowered heroines. Her mother was from the planet Naltor and possessed remarkable abilities that were passed from mother to daughter as far back as anyone could remember. One of these skills was the power to see into the future—and Nia's mother foresaw that though she would marry a human, her daughter would inherit her gifts.

Nia, a transgender woman, had thought herself exempt from this lineage, and that the superpowers would instead go to her sister, Maeve. But fate had other plans, and Nia found herself possessing powers—including astral projection, precognition, and the ability to manipulate dream energy—she never expected to.

Though still learning how to best use her many gifts, Nia has thrown herself into being a Super Hero, teaming up with Jon Kent—a.k.a. Superman—as well as his boyfriend, Jay Nakamura. With a brave heart and an unwavering dedication to do what is right, Nia fights the good fight, hoping to live up to her mother's abilities.

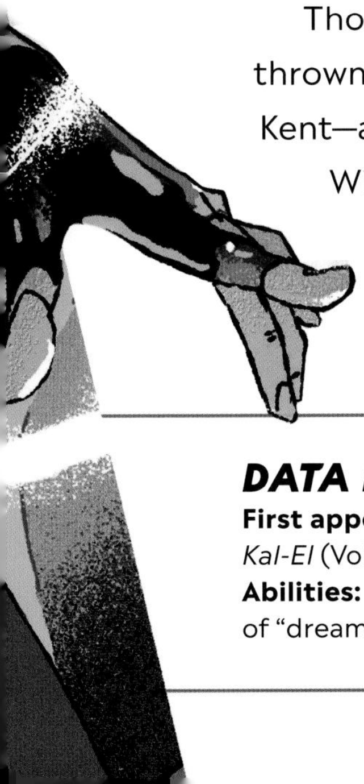

DATA FILE

First appearance: *Superman: Son of Kal-El* (Vol. 1) #13 (2022)
Abilities: Precognition, manipulation of "dream energy"
Allies: Superman (Jon Kent), Jay Nakamura, Galaxy
Likes: Campfire treats, Thursdays, the month of April

ETTA CANDY

She/her

“This isn’t work. It’s personal.”

When Wonder Woman first landed her Invisible Jet on America’s shore with Steve Trevor in tow, Etta Candy was charged with finding out who the mysterious woman was. Etta quickly realized that Wonder Woman was not a threat and became her first friend after the Amazon left Themyscira.

Etta recruited Professor Barbara Minerva to help her and Steve make Wonder Woman feel at home on Earth, and the four developed a strong bond. The dynamic between Etta and Barbara eventually turned romantic, but their feelings for each other could not survive Barbara’s transformation into Super-Villain The Cheetah.

Now a Commander, Etta continues to assist Wonder Woman in her fight against injustice and has been essential in stopping criminal masterminds such as Veronica Cale. With her trademark sense of humor, Etta is a constant reminder to Wonder Woman that even the hardest struggles can use a little of her signature catchphrase, “Woo woo!”

DATA FILE

First appearance: *Justice League* (Vol. 2) #7 (2012)
Allies: Wonder Woman, The Cheetah (Barbara Minerva), Steve Trevor
Base: Georgetown, Washington, D.C.
Likes: The poetry of Sappho

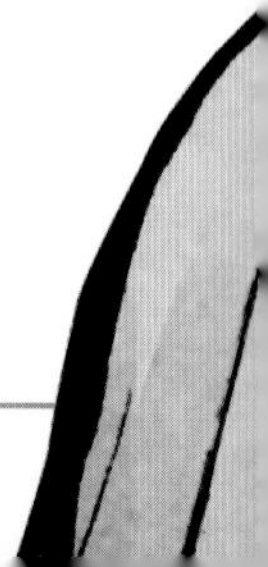

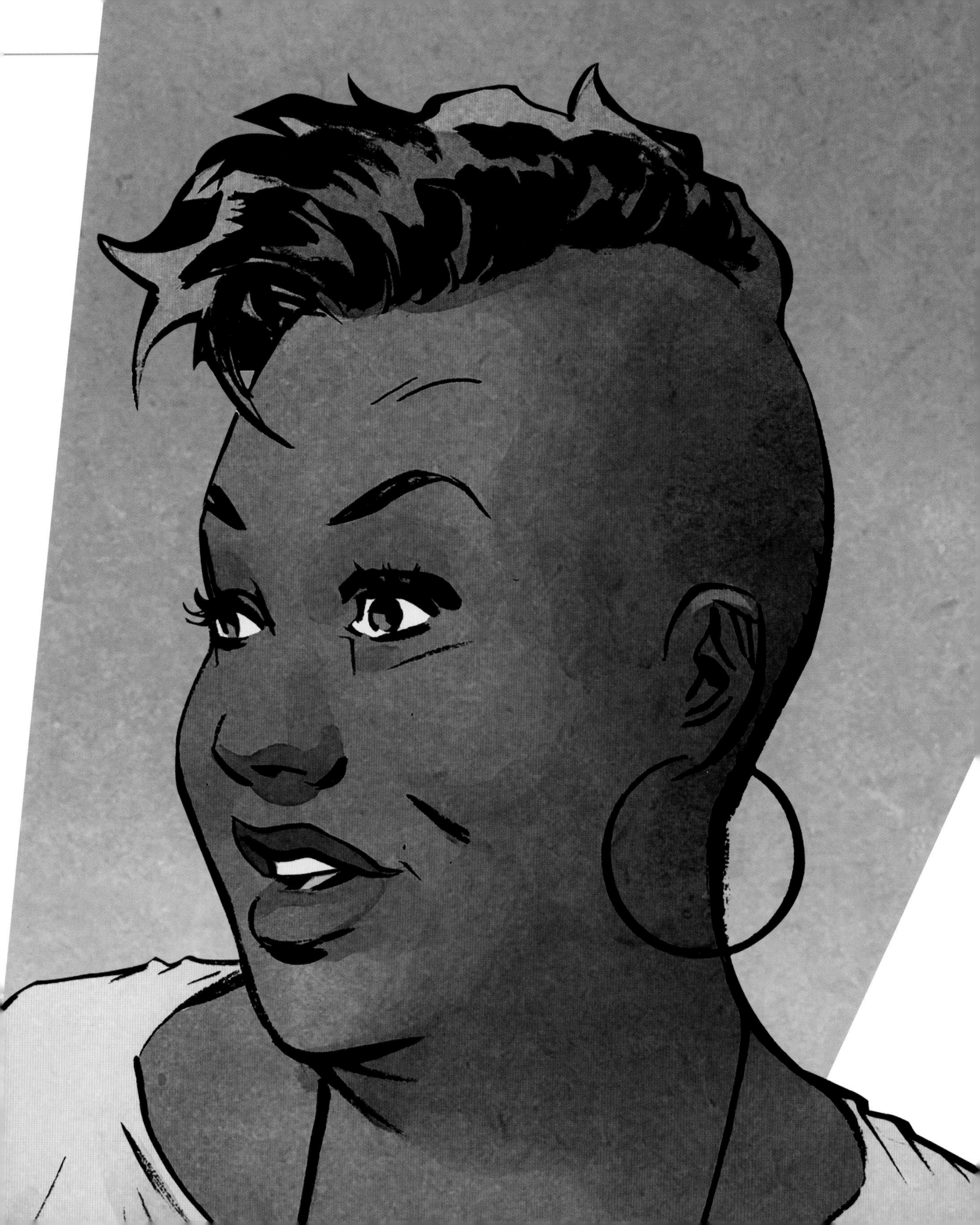

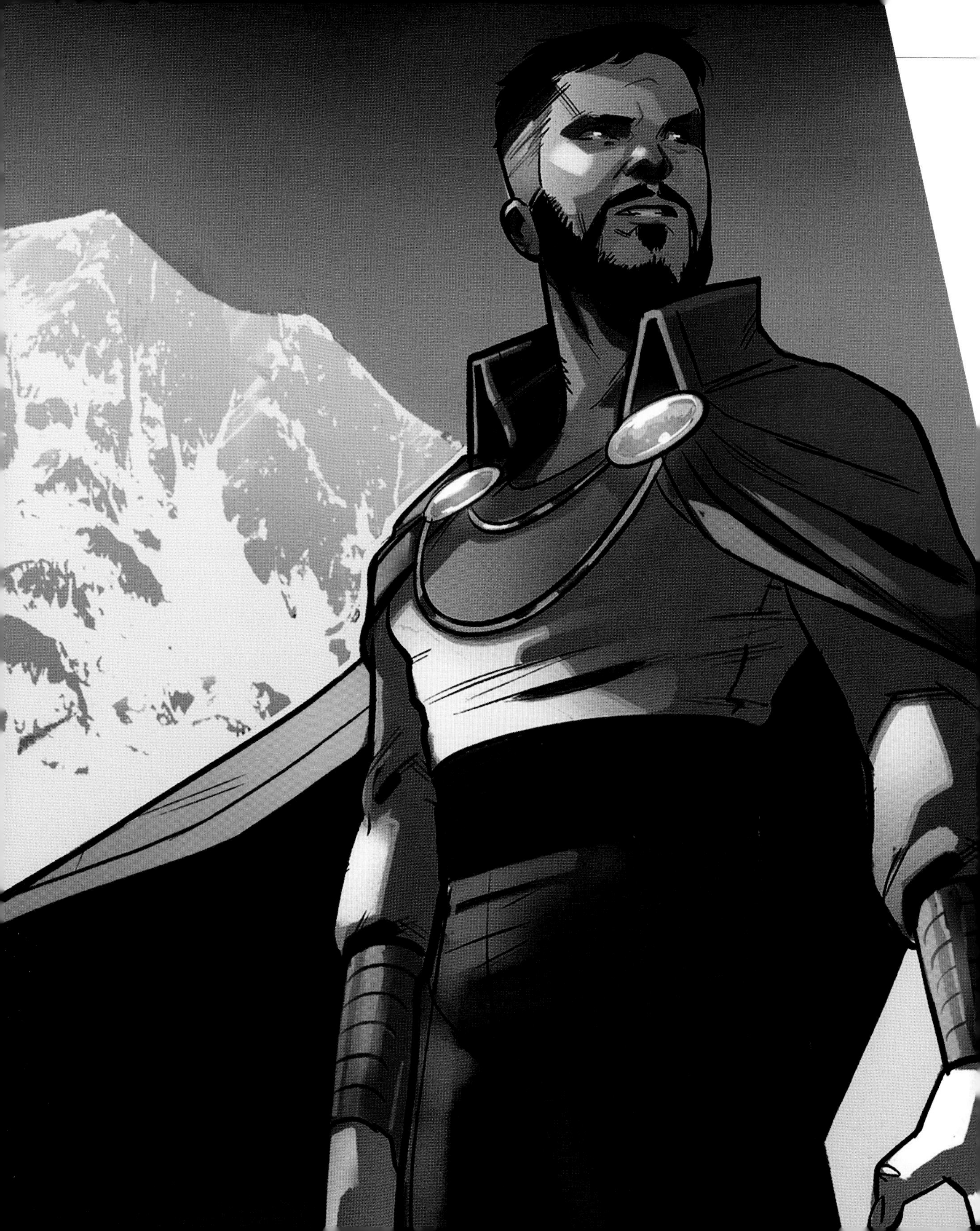

EXTRAÑO

He/him

"There's no computer for this. We've left the usual **behind** for something **decidedly 'un.'"**

Gay man and queer Super Hero elder Gregorio de la Vega spent many years studying the occult and different types of magic. Chosen by the Guardians of the Universe to be protector of Earth, Gregorio joined a Super Hero team named The New Guardians, renaming himself Extraño. Gregorio brought an earnest sense of justice and a love of life to the team. During his tenure with The New Guardians, he was diagnosed as HIV+.

Gregorio later left the Super Hero world behind and returned to his study of magic and mysticism, becoming one of the most knowledgeable practitioners in the world. He found love with his long-time partner Hugh Dawkins, who himself is the former Super Hero and Justice League member Tasmanian Devil. Together, they are raising their daughter—Suri—in Lima, Peru.

For someone who no longer considers himself a Super Hero, Gregorio keeps finding himself pulled into superheroic adventures, frequently teaming up with his friend and ally Midnighter. He has also started a social group for queer Super Heroes in the hopes that its members will never feel as alone as he once did.

DATA FILE

First appearance: *Millennium* (Vol. 1) #2 (1988)
Abilities: Magic, illusion casting, divination, levitation

Likes: Colorful scarves, tea
Dislikes: Pictures of his old extravagant costume

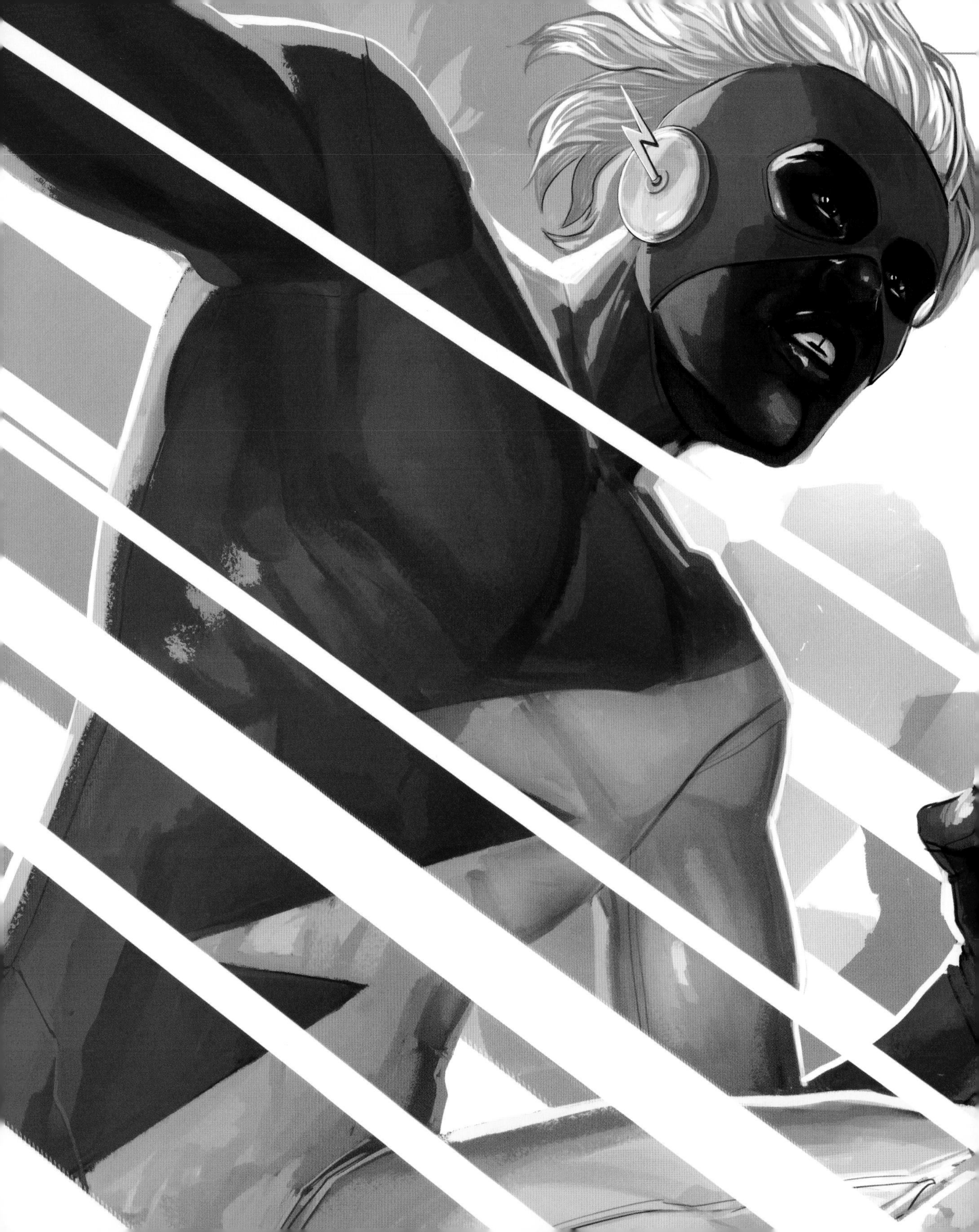

THE FLASH
(JESS CHAMBERS)
They/them

"Pretty **cool reveal,** right? I always skip to the **end,** but I **hope** you didn't."

Jess Chambers hails from an alternate earth, Earth-11, where their aunt is The Flash—the Fastest Woman Alive. Like her, Jess uses the formula $3X2(9YZ)4A$ to access the Speed Force and become super-fast. With these powers, Jess first became known as Kid Quick, teen speedster extraordinaire!

While Jess has no problem moving fast—they've even outpaced Earth-11's Superwoman—slowing down enough to get on the same page as their Teen Justice teammates is something they're still working on. This nonbinary dynamo sometimes finds the relative slowness of the world around them difficult. But they never cease to meet its collection of Super-Villains with a spring in their step.

For someone like Jess, saving just one world wasn't enough. Sometime after they joined Teen Justice, Jess learned of an oncoming threat to Earth-0, so they rushed to that world in order to warn everyone. Jess then chose to make Earth-0 their new home. This decision led to them taking on the mantle of The Flash, joining the Justice League, and dating the future Aquawoman, Andy Curry, the daughter of the first Aquaman, Arthur Curry.

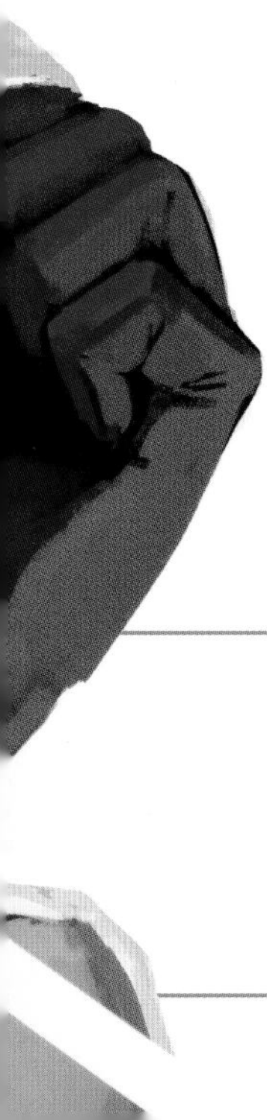

DATA FILE

First appearance: *DC's Very Merry Multiverse* (Vol. 1) #1 (2020)
Abilities: Superhuman speed, dimensional travel

Likes: Comfy sweaters, donuts, breaking the fourth wall
Dislikes: Lengthy explanations, cats (they're allergic)

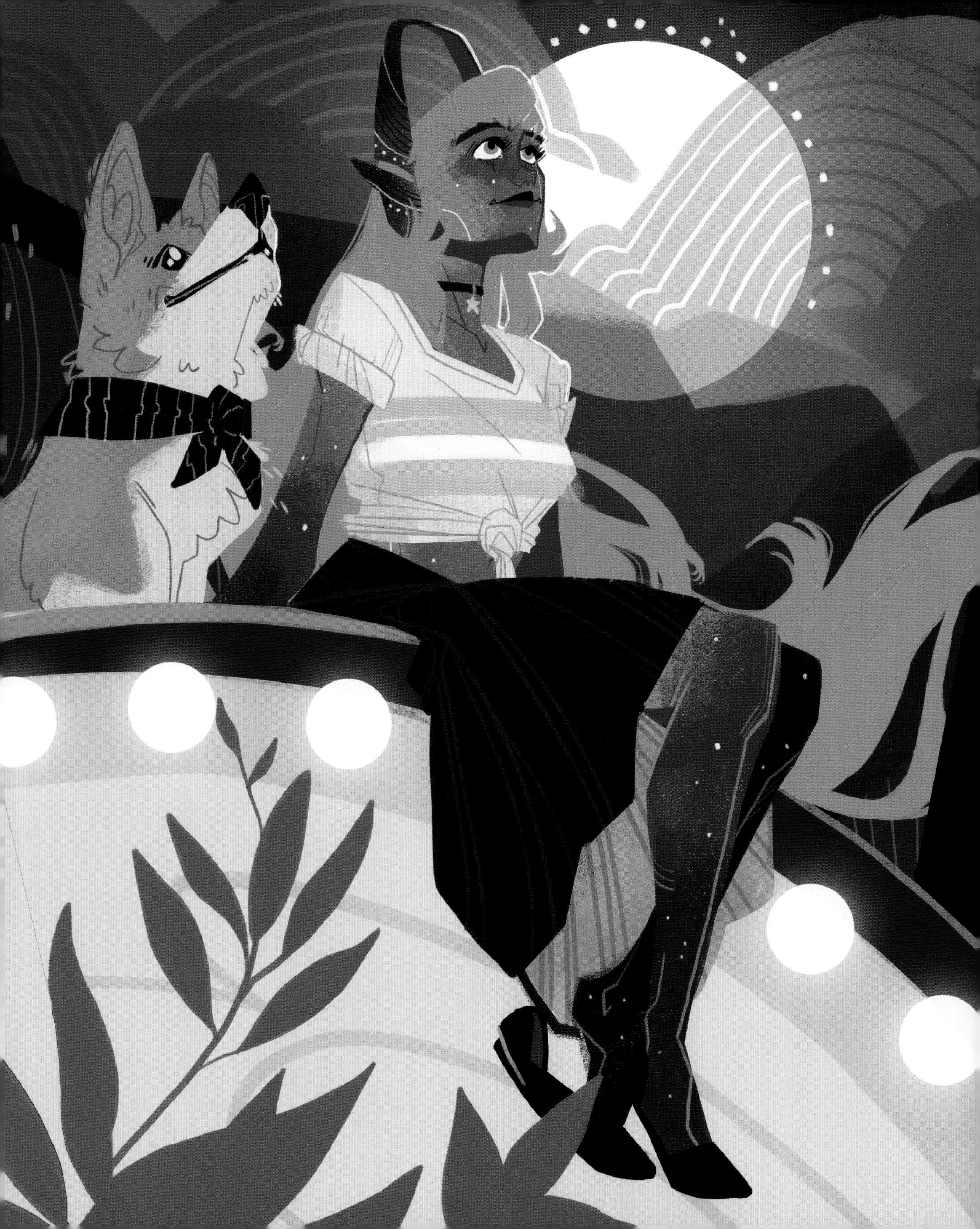

GALAXY

She/her

"Being normal was never, **never** going to save me!"

Years ago and even more light-years away, the conquering alien hive-mind known as The Vane turned their sights on the peaceful planet of Cyandii. The Queen of Cyandii gave birth in the middle of this conflict to a child, Taelyr Ilextrix-spiir Biarxiiai. When the defeat of Cyandii was imminent, the Queen's most trusted general took Taelyr and two other children and escaped to Earth to hide. In order to blend in, the general used Cyandii technology to turn himself and the three children into a human family. The general assigned Taelyr the body of a boy and the name "Taylor Barzelay."

After living nearly half her life on Earth, Taylor finally claimed her true identity at 16, becoming the superpowered alien princess she always was inside. Fully inhabiting her alien body, Taylor has found that she, like many from the planet Cyandii, can manipulate the energy and forces around her, such as gravity, heat, and electricity. Although she now feels confident in her identity as a trans lesbian, Taylor is still learning how to be a Super Hero. Fortunately, she has a lot of support from her girlfriend Kat Silverberg—who gave her the Super Hero name Galaxy—and her robotic corgi, Argus.

DATA FILE
First appearance: *Galaxy: The Prettiest Star* (2022)
Allies: Dreamer

Likes: Pickle juice, hot sauce, cuddles with Argus
Base: Ozma Gap

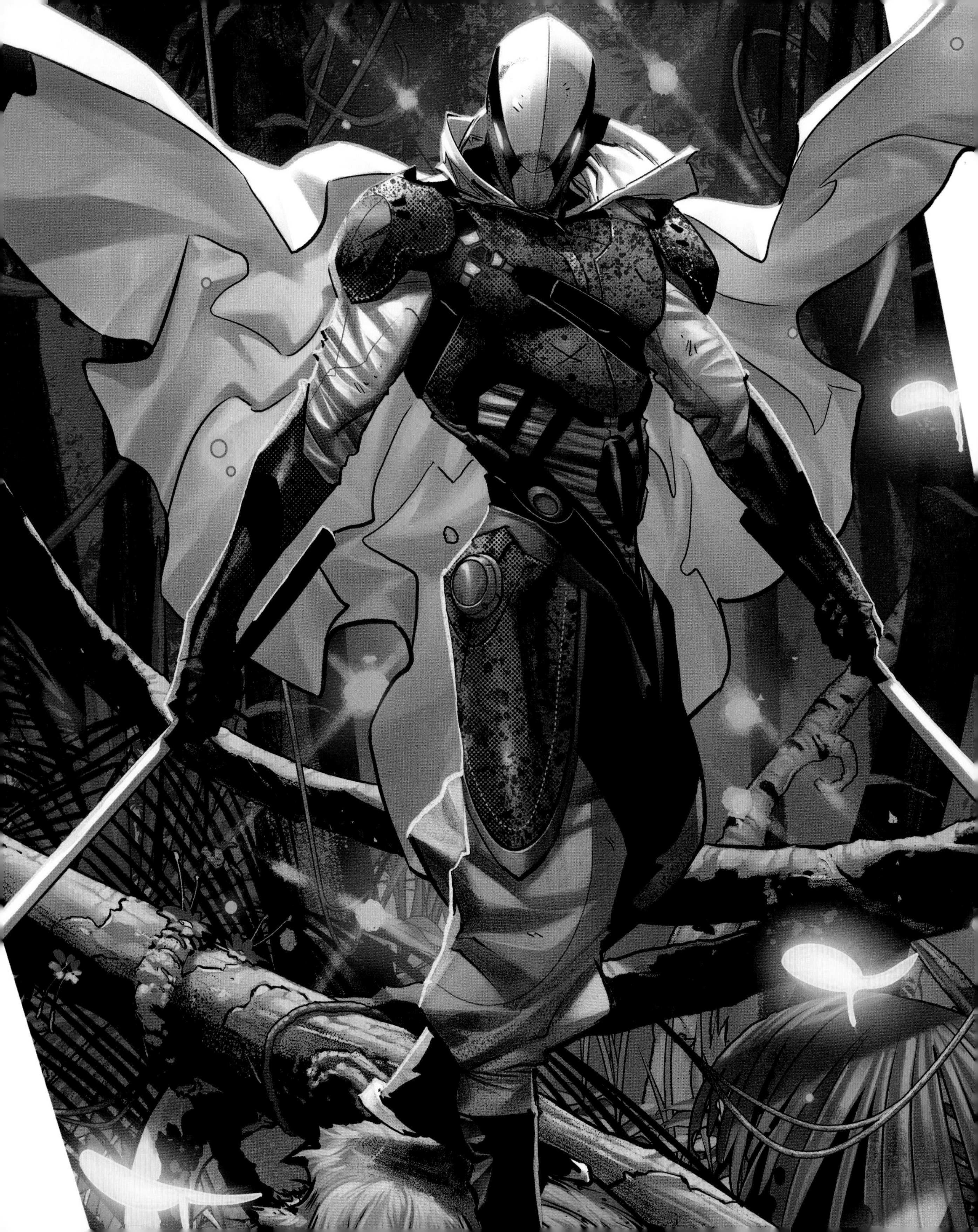

GHOST-MAKER

He/him

"The Ghost-Maker is not a man, he is a **legend.**"

Minhkhoa "Khoa" Khan trained for years to become a deadly weapon against villains everywhere, occasionally alongside a young Bruce Wayne with whom Khoa formed a friendly rivalry. Although the two boys had many of the same mentors, they had very different ideas about fighting crime. While Bruce wished to become a vigilante to avenge his parents, Khoa believed that fighting for justice was an art, and allowing emotions like grief or anger to get in the way of that was simply unacceptable.

After completing his training, Khoa began working as the vigilante Ghost-Maker. He quickly lived up to his name, showing no mercy to any criminals he came across. Disappointed by the way that Bruce was handling crime in Gotham City as Batman, Khoa eventually arrived to show him how it should be done.

Batman agreed to let his old rival help—on the condition that he did not kill anyone. Never one to resist a challenge, Khoa agreed. Ghost-Maker now operates as part of Batman's ever-increasing family and leads the international crime-fighting team Batman Incorporated. While this queer vigilante has had many partners of many genders over the years, his true love will always remain the art of fighting crime.

DATA FILE

First appearance: *Batman* (Vol. 3) #100 (2020)
Allies: Batman, Harley Quinn, Clownhunter, Oracle, Gray Wolf

Abilities: Acrobatics, computer hacking, martial arts
Dislikes: Showing his face, emotions in general

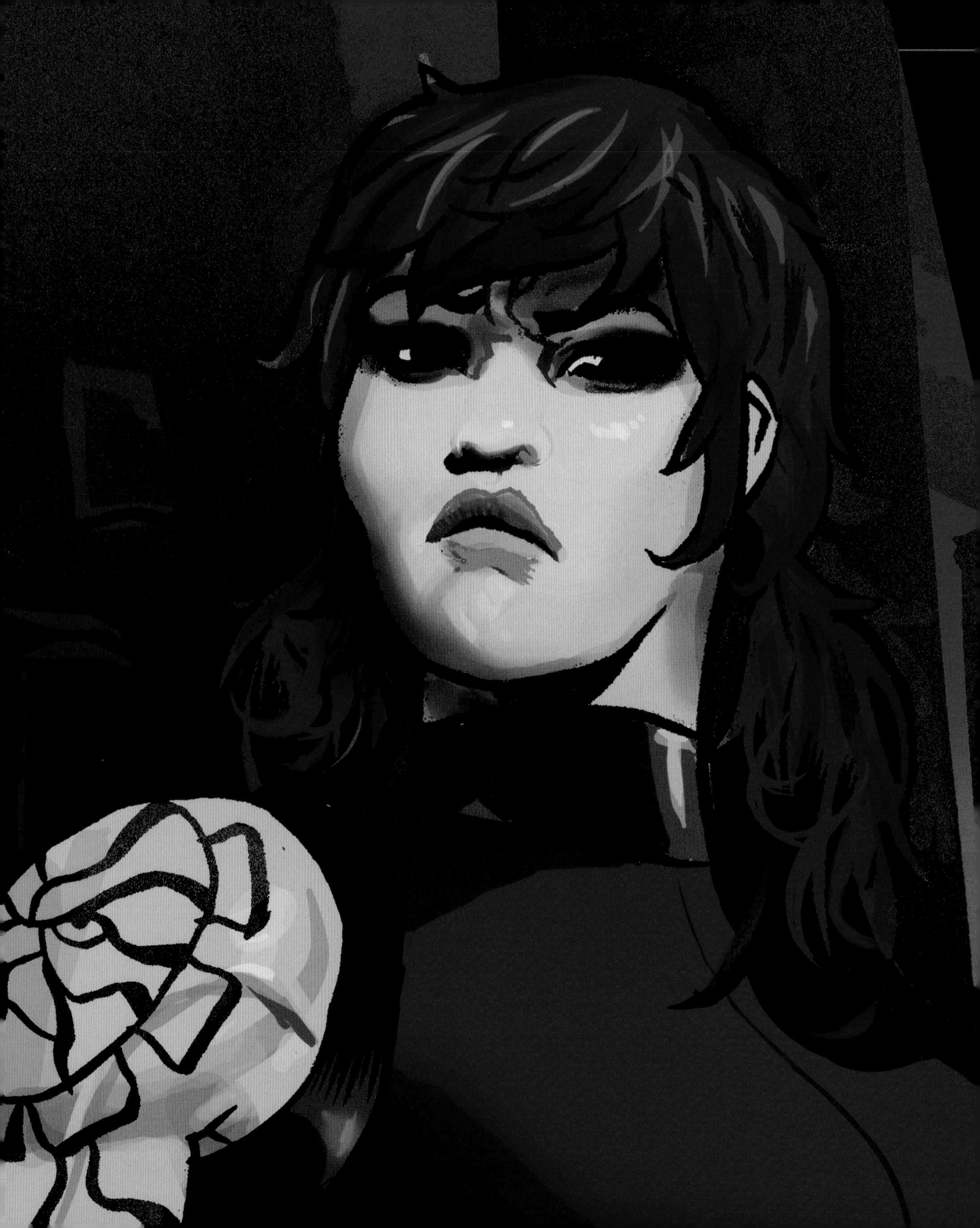

GRACE CHOI

She/her

"Grace is my name, **not my manner!**"

Grace Choi has always had trouble fitting in. The seven-foot-tall bisexual daughter of a Korean father and an Amazonian mother, Grace grew up in several foster homes before running away at the age of nine. Although this was a harrowing time in Grace's life, she survived thanks to her Amazonian abilities.

Grace spent her teenage years in underground fighting tournaments, before eventually becoming a bouncer at a nightclub for superhumans in Metropolis. It was during this time that she was asked to join the Super Hero team the Outsiders, and while she initially turned down the offer, she quickly changed her mind when she found out how much she would be paid.

In her early days with the Outsiders, Grace often clashed with other team members, who found her brash attitude difficult to deal with. But over time, she formed close bonds with her teammates, particularly Anissa Pierce—the Super Hero known as Thunder. Their initial bickering eventually changed into genuine affection—which then led to romance. Grace may still not know where she fits in, but at least she knows who she fits in with.

DATA FILE

First appearance: *Outsiders* (Vol. 3) #1 (2003)

Allies: Thunder, Arsenal, Nightwing,

Likes: Family sitcoms, hair dye, budae jjigae

Dislikes: Mornings, wearing T-shirts,

GREEN ARROW
(CONNOR HAWKE)
He/him

"Hatred is not the answer to fear.
Your fear is your weakness."

Connor Hawke is the son of Oliver Queen—also known as the Super Hero Green Arrow. Although Connor grew up never knowing his father, he followed Green Arrow's adventures on the news, and at the age of 13, he joined the Buddhist ashram where Green Arrow had once stayed. There, he became a master of Aikido and a skilled Kyudo archer.

When Oliver returned to the ashram, he found Connor, and the two began making up for lost time. Oliver and his buddy Eddie Fyers would try to bond with Connor by talking about their favorite subject—women—but Connor showed no interest, often causing distance between him and his father.

Unfortunately, not long after the men were reunited, Oliver died saving the city of Metropolis, and Connor continued his father's legacy by becoming the new Green Arrow. When Oliver came back to life, he and Connor decided to share the mantle of Green Arrow and fight side by side. Now grown out of his father's shadow, Connor is working on both embracing his asexuality and figuring out his own path to being a great hero.

DATA FILE
First appearance: *Green Arrow* (Vol. 2) #0 (1994)
Allies: Green Arrow (Oliver Queen), Green Lantern (Kyle Rayner), Robin (Damian Wayne), Black Canary
Likes: Rejecting materialism—except for ice cream
Dislikes: Uncomfortable shoes, Christmas shopping

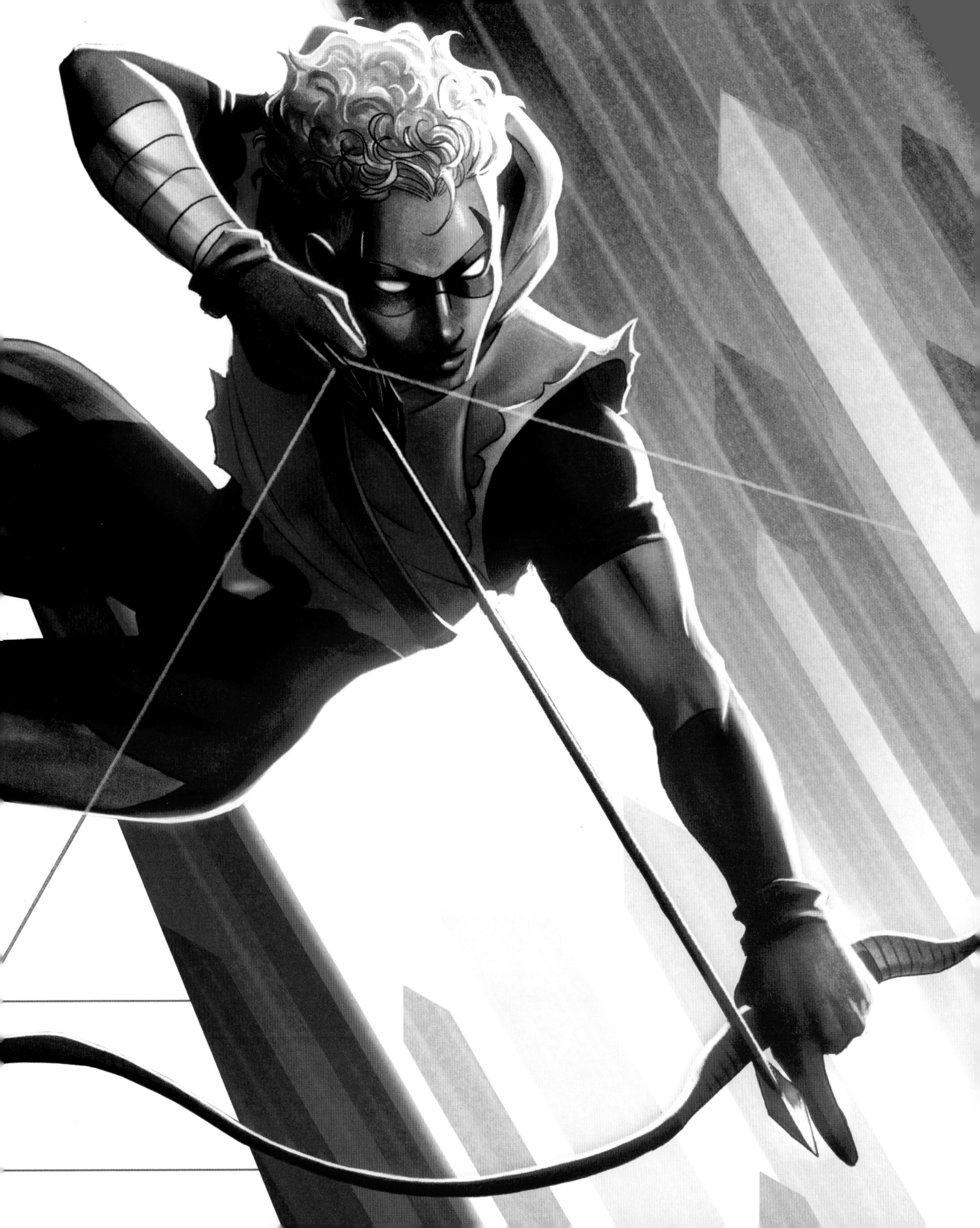

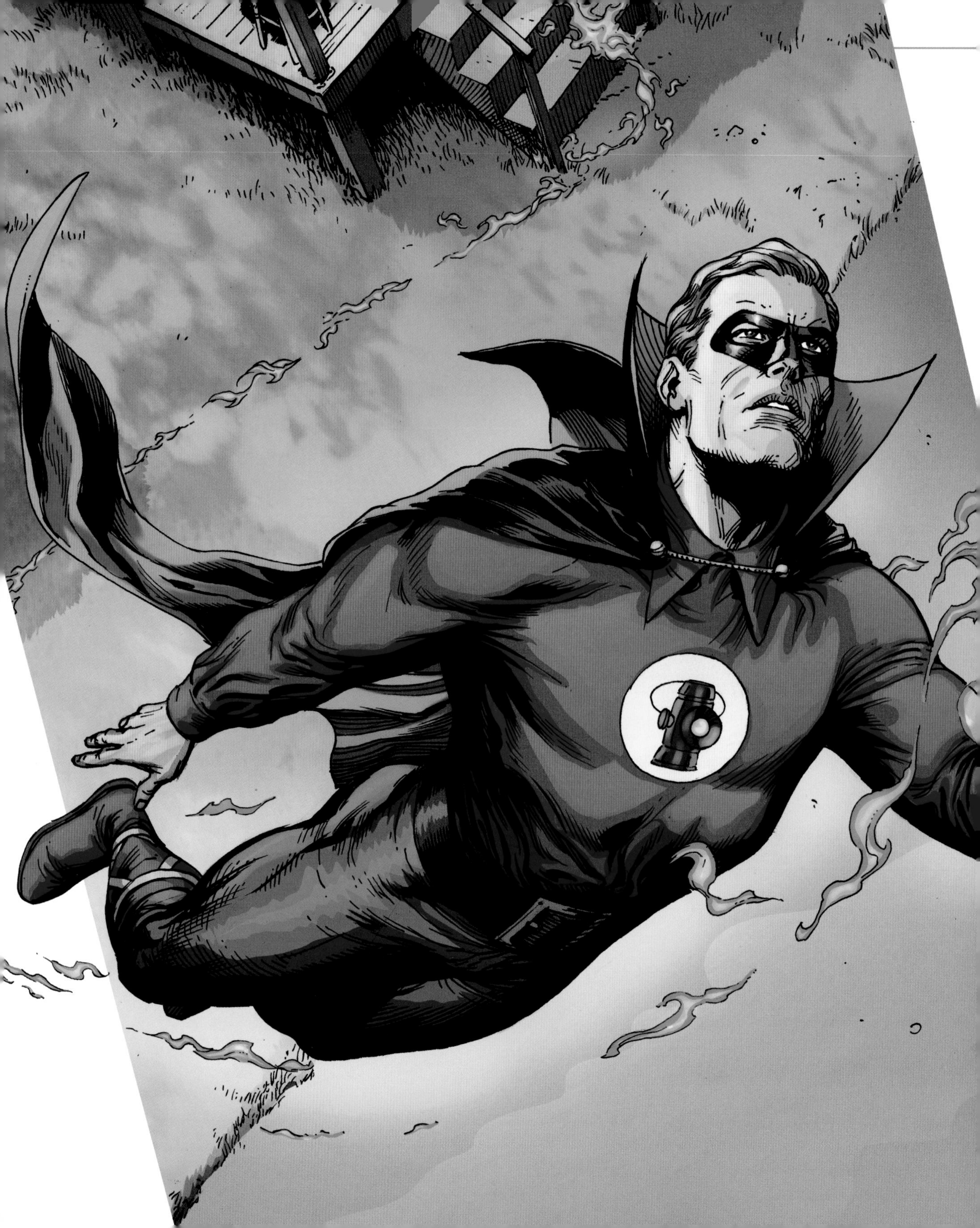

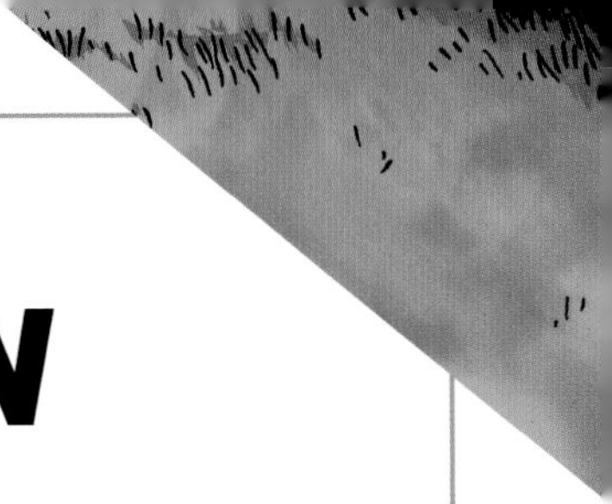

GREEN LANTERN
(ALAN SCOTT)

He/him

"I promise you I know how dark things can get when you keep emotions secret."

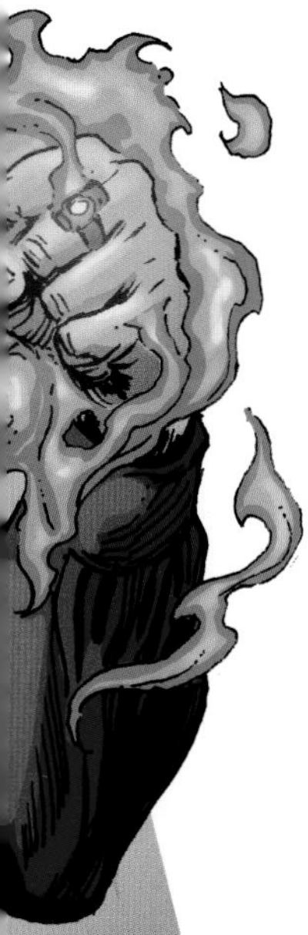

One of the world's first Super Heroes, Alan Scott is no stranger to secret identities—as well as fighting crime under a masked alias, he also spent many years hiding that he is a gay man. Before becoming a Super Hero, Alan attempted to run away with his boyfriend, Jimmy, but the train they were on was sabotaged and crashed. A strange, mystic force known as the Starheart saved Alan and gave him incredible power, focused in a ring that Alan had intended to give to Jimmy. Wearing the ring, Alan became the Green Lantern, a fiery beacon of hope and justice in a dark world. He became a founding member of the Justice Society of America, the world's first Super Hero team.

After the accident, Alan never spoke of his love for Jimmy or his sexuality. He married the reformed Super-Villain The Thorn and had two children with her. Once the kids reached adulthood, they became Super Heroes themselves: Obsidian and Jade.

Recently, Alan came out as a gay man to his children and peers. After receiving an overwhelmingly positive response, Alan finally feels ready to live his life in all its brightness.

DATA FILE

First appearance: *All-American Comics* (Vol. 1) #16 (1940)
Allies: Obsidian, Jade, The Flash (Jay Garrick), Wildcat (Ted Grant), Hawkman (Carter Hall)
Base: Gotham City
Likes: Detective novels, ham on rye sandwiches

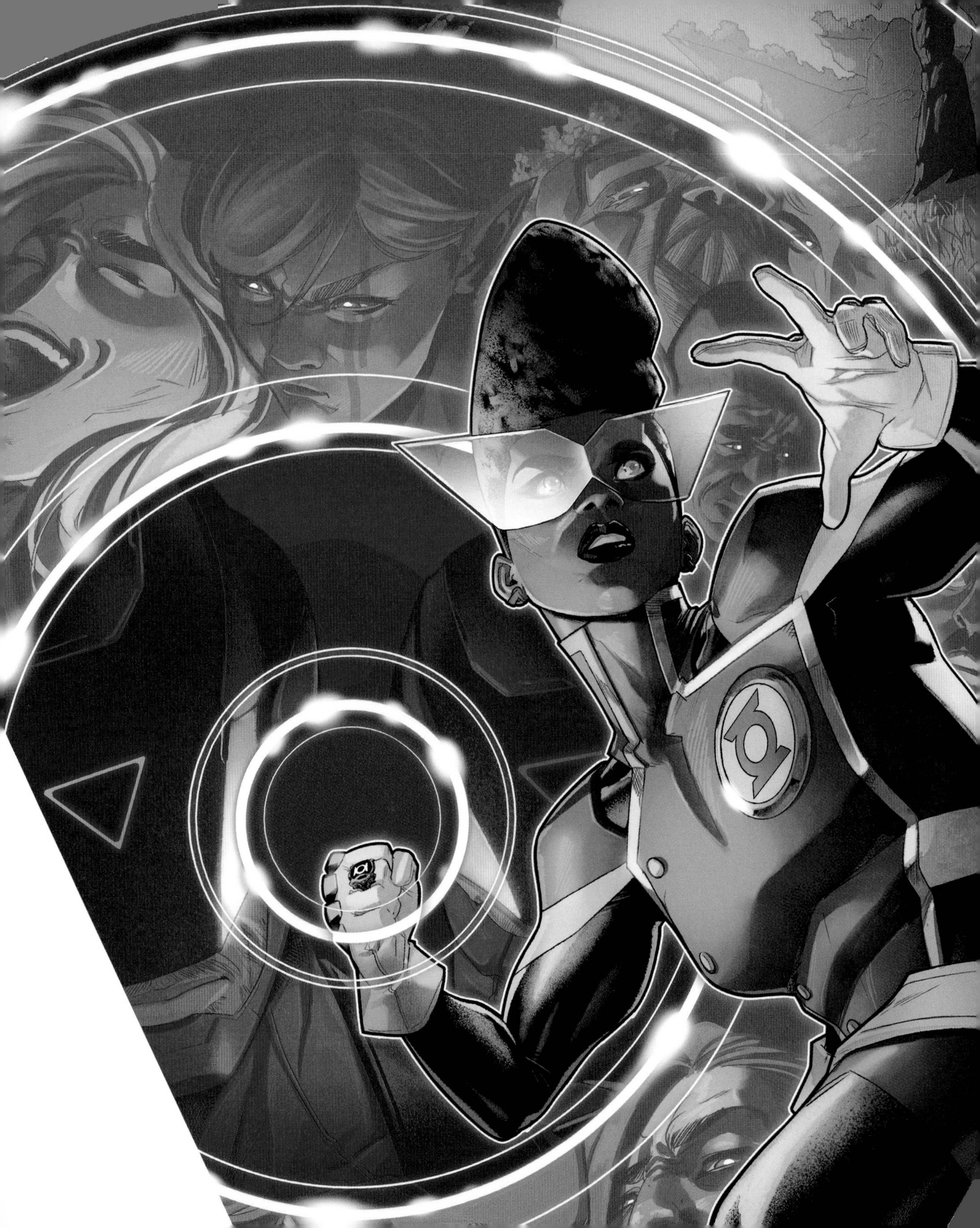

GREEN LANTERN
(SOJOURNER MULLEIN)
She/her

"Nobody here has a clue about how to handle all of this. Except me. Welcome to Far Sector."

From a young age, Sojourner "Jo" Mullein was determined to make a difference. It was this determination that led to Jo becoming a police officer. Unfortunately, instead of justice, all Jo found was oppression. When she witnessed a colleague violently attacking a suspect, Jo did the right thing and reported him— only to be fired while their superiors backed him instead.

It was at this low moment that a rogue Guardian of the Universe saw in Jo a strong will—one that far outstripped any Green Lantern's. This Guardian gave Jo a special power ring. With this ring, Jo was finally able to fight for change. She became the Green Lantern of Far Sector and worked with the alien citizens of the City Enduring, solving the first murder they had had in 500 years. Openly bisexual, Jo has also dated some of its residents, including Marth of the Sea and Syzn of the Cliffs.

After the Central Power Battery of Oa—the Green Lanterns' source of energy—implodes, Jo is one of the few Lanterns left with a working power ring. With it, she leads the investigation into the incident and restores balance to Oa. Now Jo stands with her fellow Lanterns, and the galaxy is safer for it.

DATA FILE
First appearance: *Far Sector* (Vol. 1) #1 (2020)
Allies: Green Lantern (Simon Baz), The Flash (Jess Chambers), Superman (Jon Kent)
Abilities: Creating anything she imagines out of green light
Likes: Fanfiction, giant robot anime, coffee

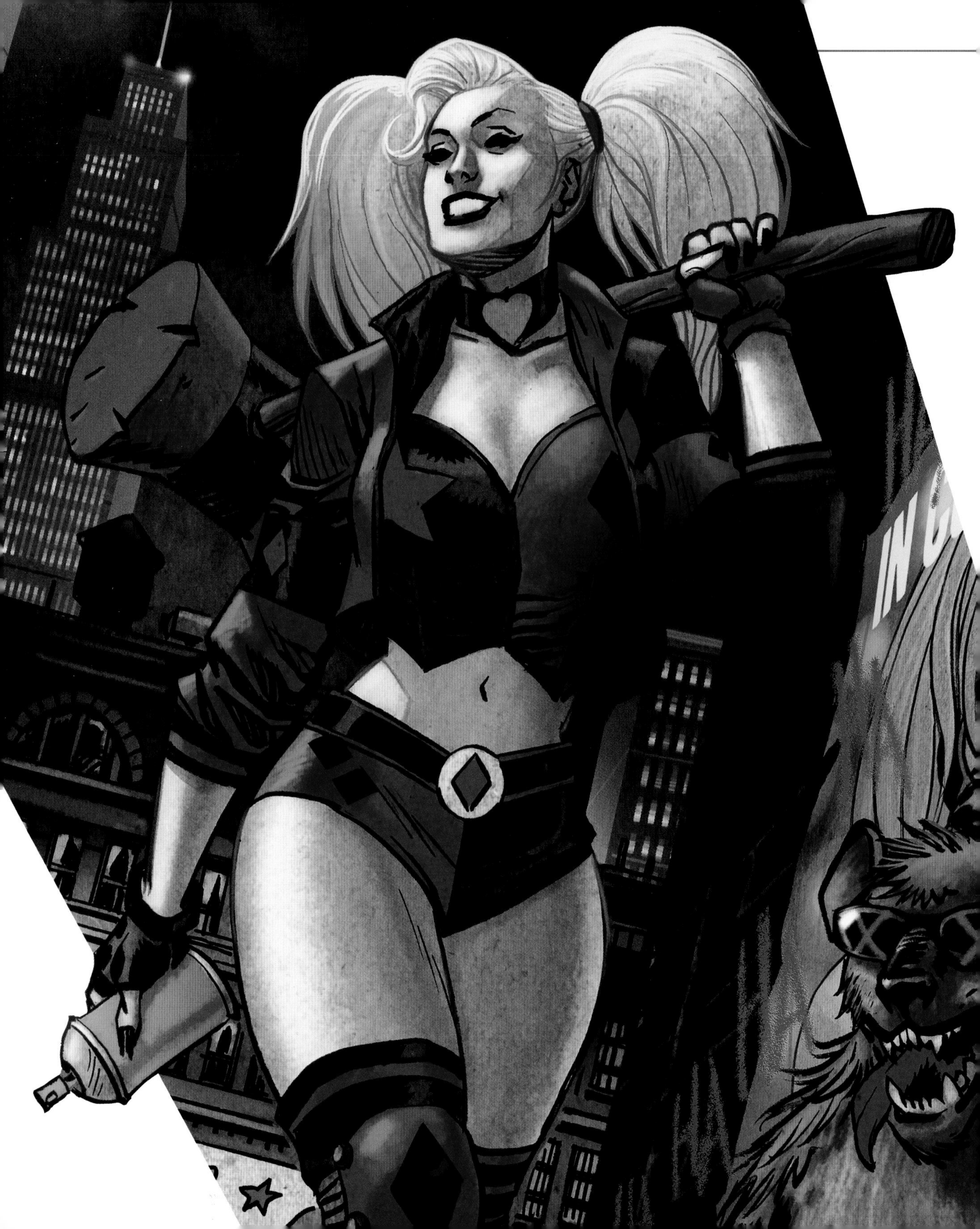

IN

HARLEY QUINN

She/her

"I mean, if you're gonna be evil, at least make it interestin'."

Criminal psychiatrist Harleen Quinzel thought she knew it all... until she met The Joker. Her time with the Clown Prince of Crime unlocked a streak of madness and unpredictability that rivaled even his. As Harley Quinn, she helped The Joker cause a crime wave the likes of which Gotham City had never seen, but their relationship—while often electric—was toxic and completely unsustainable.

Harley kicked The Joker to the curb and struck out on her own as a Super-Villain to be reckoned with. As time went by, her frequent partner-in-crime Poison Ivy became a partner-in-everything-else. Even if they don't always agree with each other's methods, their love will always bring them back together.

After a stint in the Suicide Squad, Harley made her most unpredictable move yet—she renounced her villainous past and has tried to do good with the Batman Family. But you can't keep this Clown Queen of Crime out of trouble for long, and she's been itching to get into some fresh mayhem...

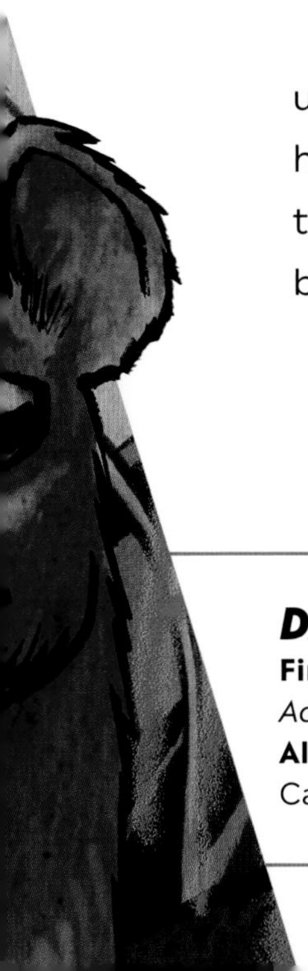

DATA FILE

First appearance: *The Batman Adventures* (Vol. 1) #12 (1993)
Allies: Poison Ivy, Power Girl, Catwoman, Batman
Likes: Her pet hyenas, hitting things with a giant mallet
Dislikes: Matching shoes, being underestimated, The Joker

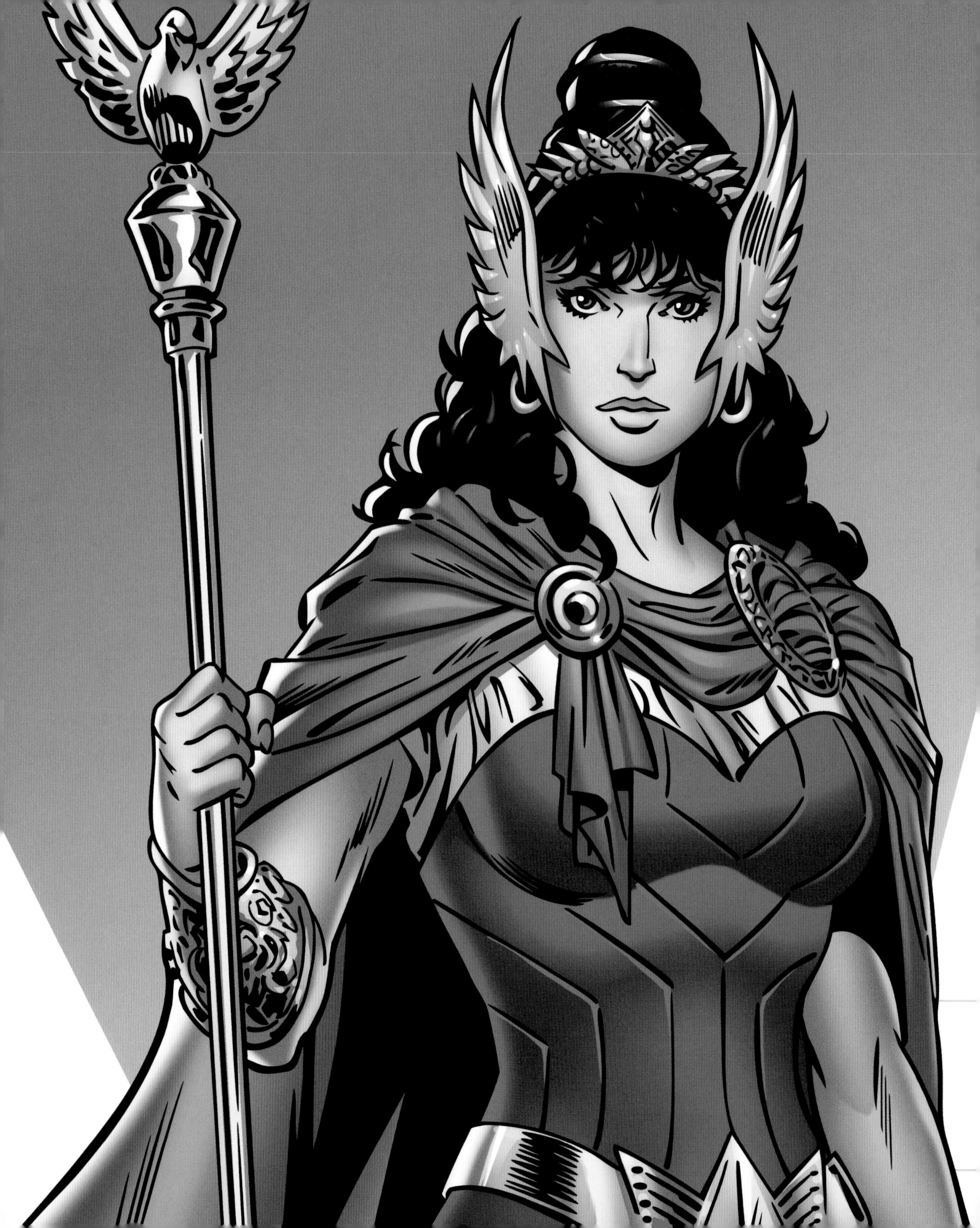

HIPPOLYTA

She/her

"I am **Hippolyta!** Does **anyone** else here **challenge us?!**"

Hippolyta was the first Amazon to emerge from the Well of Souls, reborn as a powerful warrior. As more of her Amazonian sisters came from the Well, Hippolyta led them in turning Themyscira—the island created for her and the Amazonians—into a paradise. Building a new society based on sisterhood and the celebration of martial arts, the warriors chose Hippolyta to be their queen.

Centuries later, Hippolyta longed for a child, and begged the gods to bless her with one. Her wish was granted with a daughter, Diana. Princess Diana became the Amazons' greatest champion and was sent out from Themyscira as the Super Hero Wonder Woman.

Hippolyta herself took on the mantle of Wonder Woman at times when Diana could not, allying herself with the Justice Society of America and the Justice League. But her home would always be on Themyscira with her fellow Amazons—particularly her chief counselor, Philippus. Hippolyta and Philippus are the loves of each other's immortal lives, and both women consider themselves mothers to Diana.

DATA FILE
First appearance: *All Star Comics* (Vol. 1) #8 (1941)
Allies: Wonder Woman, Nubia, Philippus, Antiope

Likes: Archery, horse-riding, dates soaked in honey

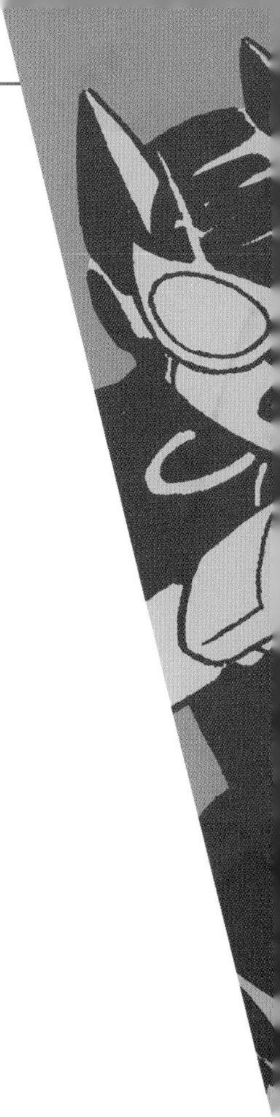

HOLLY ROBINSON

She/her

"What would the real Catwoman do? Besides steal something, I mean."

Holly Robinson spent much of her early life running away—first from her parents, then from the dangers that came with growing up as a homeless youth. She only realized that fighting back was a possibility after being saved from a cop by another teenager named Selina Kyle. Holly stopped running and stayed with Selina, who became her mentor and protector.

Years later, when Selina took on the mantle of Catwoman, Holly acted as her assistant by helping her plan heists. Selina eventually decided to take a break from being Catwoman, and she asked Holly to take her place. Holly attempted to use the Catwoman identity for more heroic pursuits, but was forced to abandon it after her secret identity was revealed to the public.

Selina helped Holly once again when she encouraged her to ask out Karon, a young woman working at a corner deli. Holly took her friend's advice, forming a relationship with Karon that eventually led to them moving in together. Finally, Holly found a safe place to call home.

DATA FILE

First appearance: *Batman* (Vol. 1) #404 (1987)
Allies: Catwoman, Harley Quinn
Likes: Cats, corner stores, short hair
Dislikes: Authority figures, busybodies

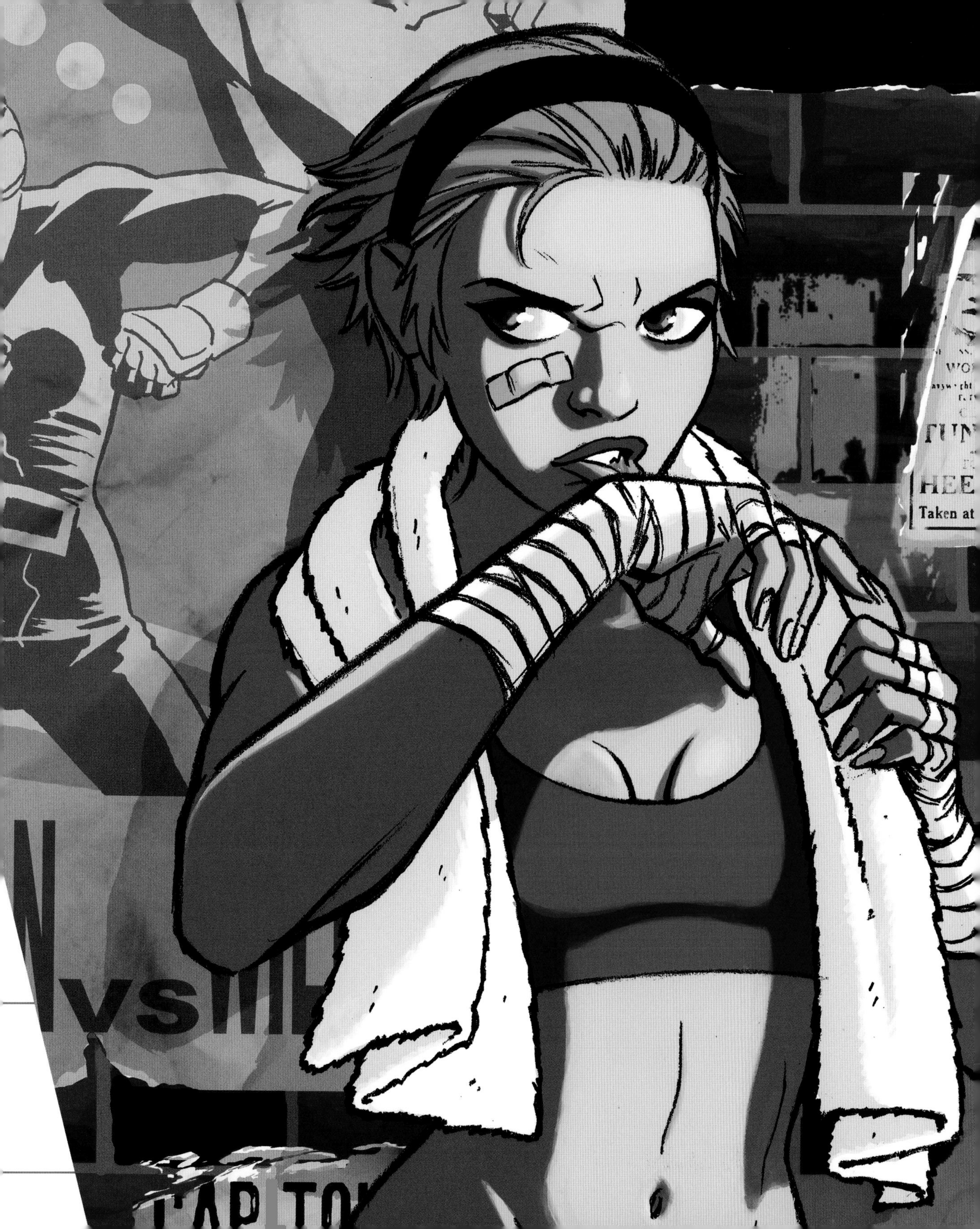
Taken at
vs

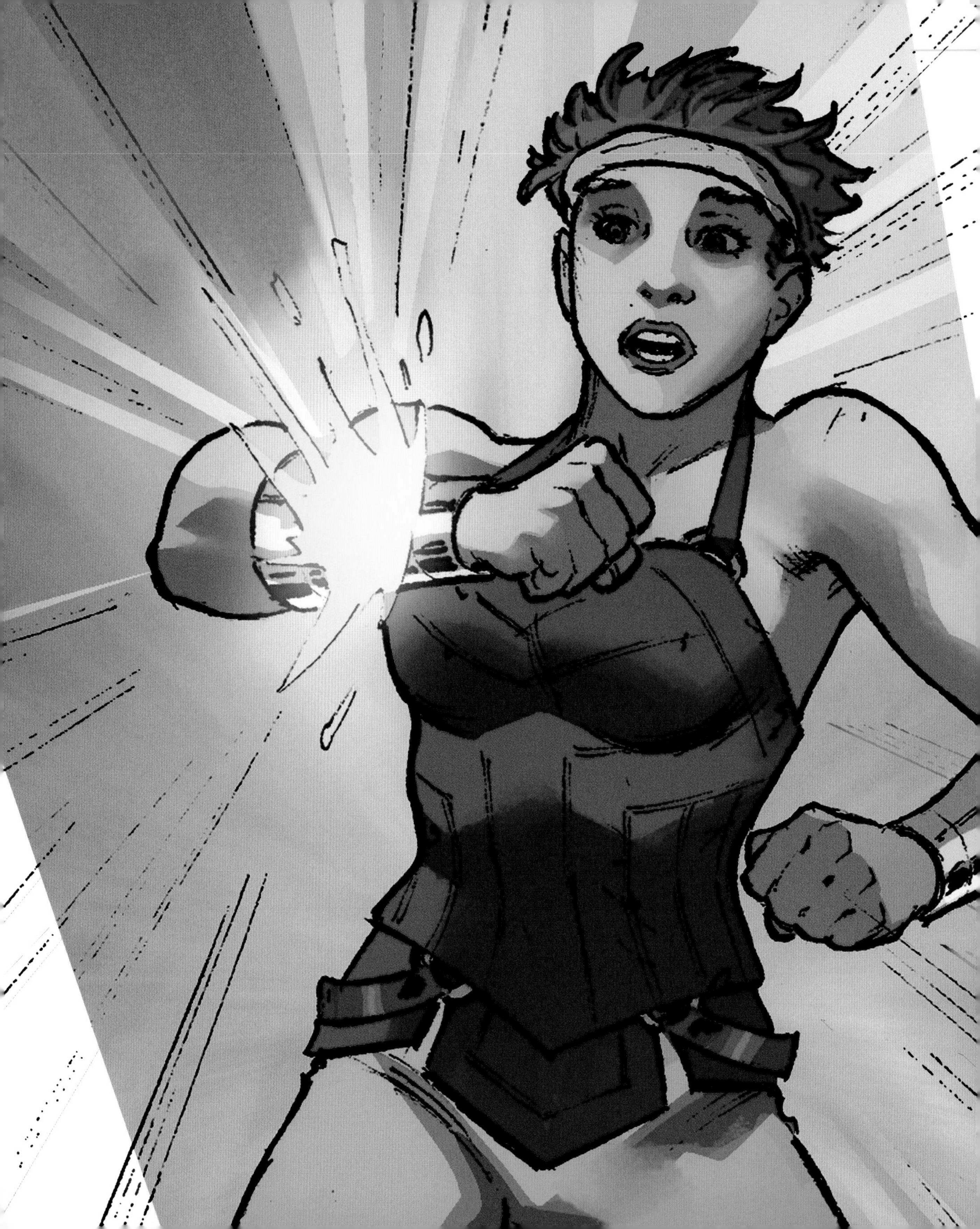

Io

She/her

"The power that manifests from almost any weapon ultimately comes from its wielder."

Io has always known how to build things. Instead of fighting in battle like many of her Amazon sisters, she uses her strong arms and skilled hands to create beautiful—but deadly—weapons and armor for them. Ever since she was reborn from the Well of Souls, Io has fulfilled this role happily.

Perhaps more than any Amazon, Io pines for love. Without any heroic victories to call her own, bashful Io found it difficult to act on her own desires. For many years, she harbored feelings for Wonder Woman, and even joined her at a Themyscira embassy in Washington, D.C.. But if Wonder Woman knew of those feelings, she never spoke of them—and neither did Io.

While things may not have been destined to work out with Wonder Woman, Io eventually caught the attention of Nubia. The beautiful new Queen of the Amazons was drawn to Io's gentle nature and incredible talent—and had no problem letting Io know. The two of them have now forged a connection stronger than any sword Io could ever create.

DATA FILE

First appearance: *Wonder Woman* (Vol. 2) #196 (2003)
Allies: Nubia, Wonder Woman, Hippolyta
Likes: Sunsets, the sound of the ocean, a clean workshop
Dislikes: People who don't care for their tools, indoor plants

JAY NAKAMURA

He/him

"I'm the **one person** in the world you don't have to worry about."

Jay Nakamura is a brave and strong-willed activist. A refugee from the island nation of Gamorra, he puts his journalism skills to good use by running his own underground activist group, The Truth, breaking stories on its news website that the mainstream media doesn't report, such as the treatment of people from his country.

He was experimented on by the Post-Human Project, an illegal enterprise implemented by Henry Bendix, Gamorra's president at the time. Jay gained the power of intangibility—meaning he can move through solid objects. With his new skill, Jay escaped Bendix's clutches and began a new life in Metropolis. But Bendix's reign of terror seemed to follow Jay, and he found himself and his loved ones threatened once again.

Fortunately, this young man has powerful loved ones, particularly Jon Kent—also known as Superman. The two met at Metropolis College when Jon saved Jay's life, and their mutual attraction soon became a loving relationship. Jon and Jay are both determined to stand up for truth and justice, which makes them an incredible team.

DATA FILE

First appearance: *Superman: Son of Kal-El* (Vol. 1) #2 (2021)
Allies: Superman (Jon Kent), The Aerie, Wink, Dreamer

Likes: Capes, farmers markets, the Metropolis hot dog
Dislikes: Smog, people who cut in line, most dinosaurs

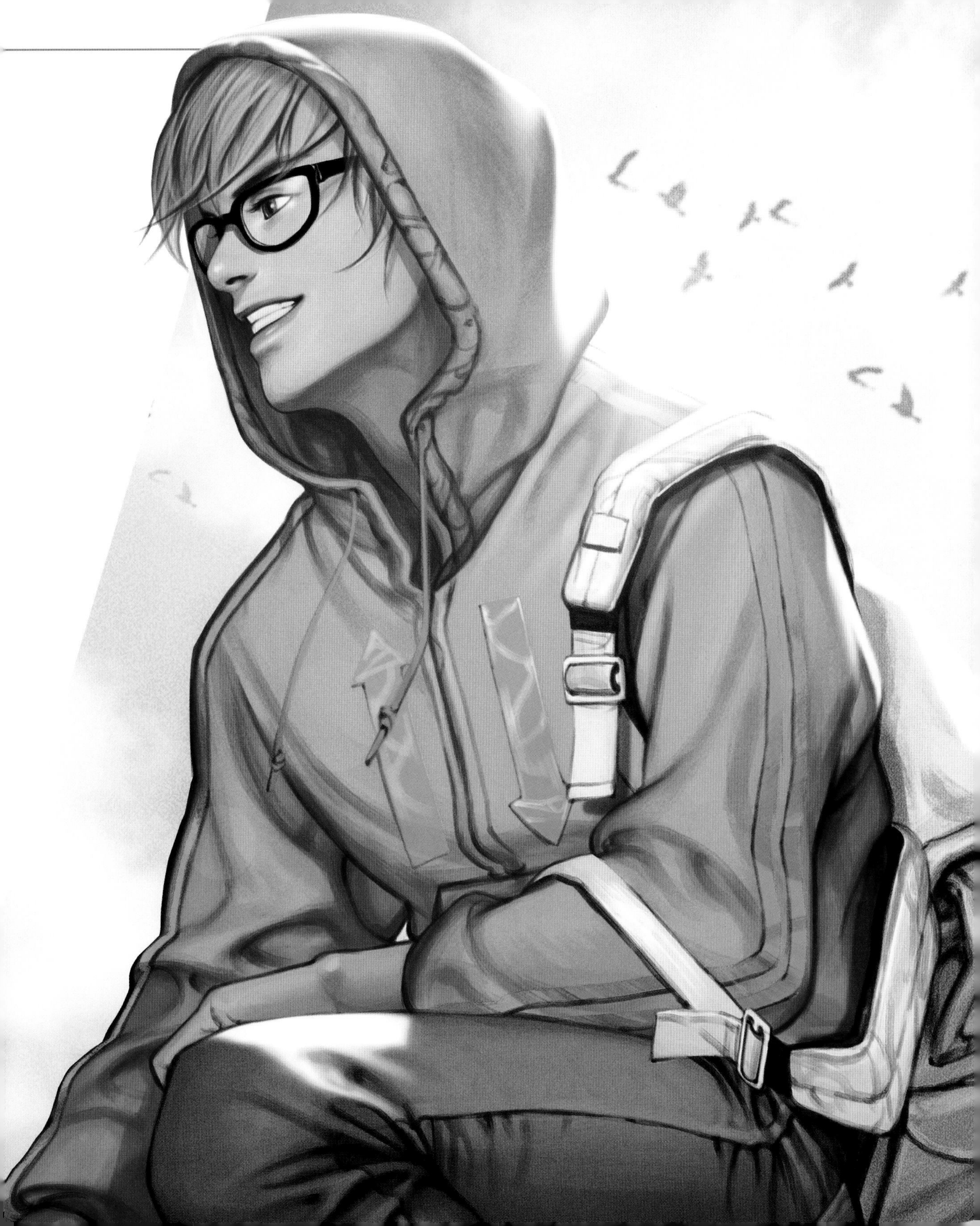

JERICHO

He/him

"We've focused so much on what's out here—what's beyond the **stars**—we miss the point that there are infinite universes in here—inside our **minds!**"

As a son of the Super-Villain Deathstroke, Joseph "Joey" Wilson's life was always filled with danger. When he was a child, Joey was almost killed by one of his father's foes. While Joey survived, it left him unable to speak. After his mother found out what had happened, she took him and his brother away.

Unfortunately, Joey could not escape his father forever. As a result of experiments that Deathstroke carried out on him when he was younger, Joey has the ability to jump inside other people's minds and control their bodies. When Deathstroke was hired to destroy the Teen Titans, Joey decided to help the young Super Heroes. Joey saved his new friends and then joined the team, calling himself Jericho.

While Joey refuses to label his sexuality, he has been in relationships with men and women. One relationship was with David Isherwood, a genius who created a device that allows Joey to "talk" to anyone who has the receiver. While their relationship ended in tragedy, Joey survived, continuing to fight another day.

DATA FILE

First appearance: *Tales of the Teen Titans* (Vol. 1) #42 (1984)
Allies: Ravager, Raven, Kole
Likes: The latest release of any gadget, healthy boundaries, Christmas
Dislikes: Annual checkups, explosions

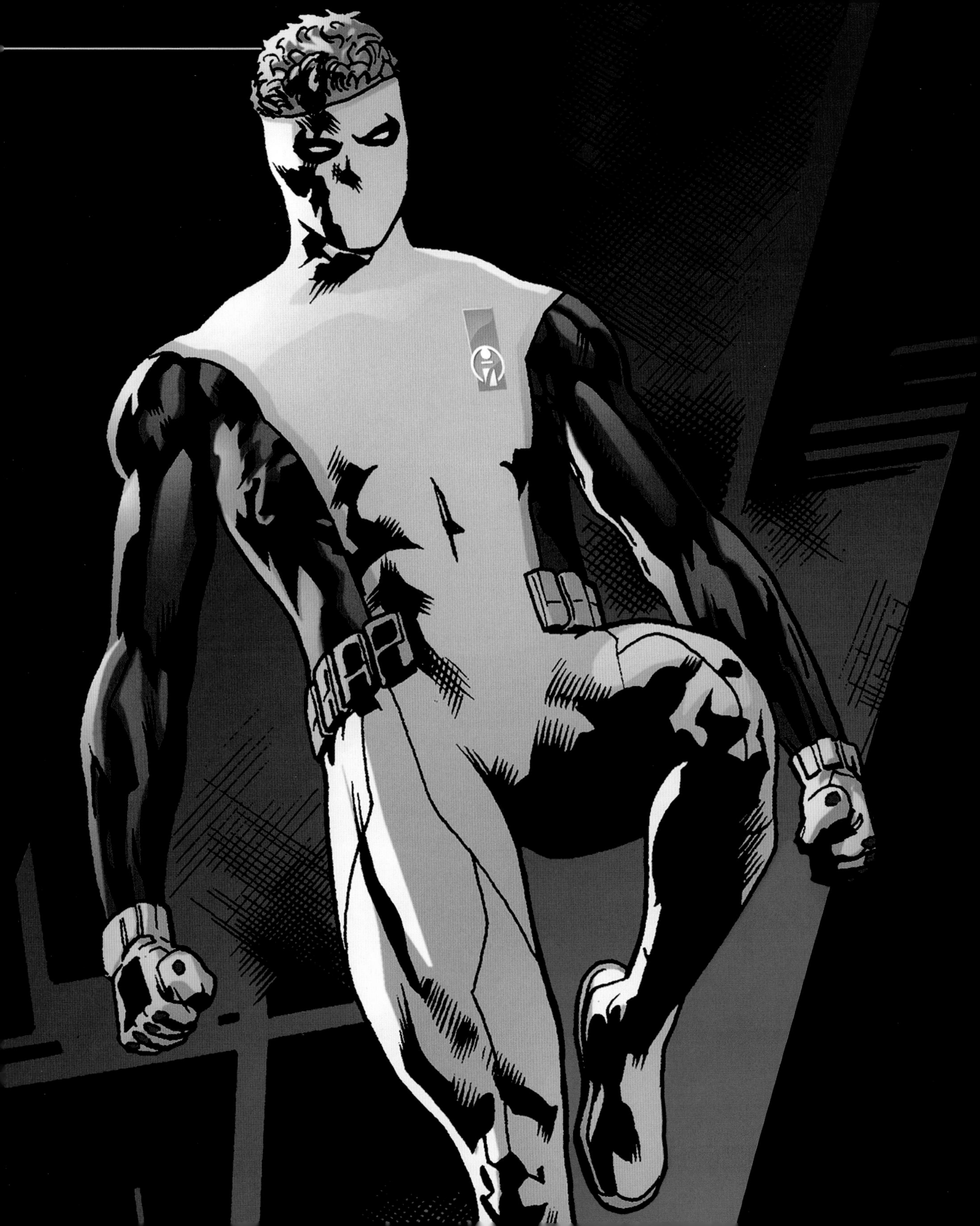

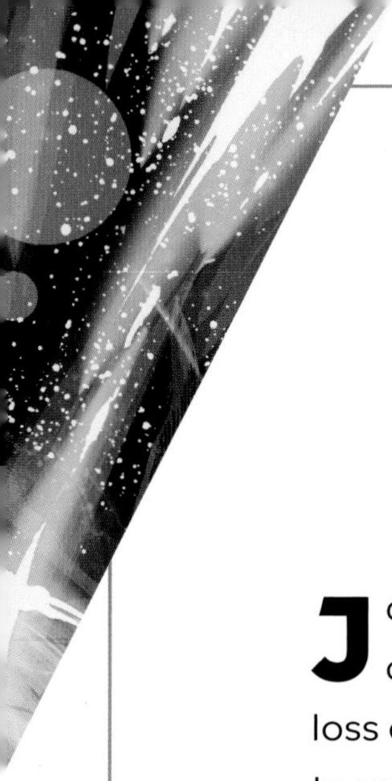

JOHN CONSTANTINE

He/him

"I'm a nasty piece of work, Chief."

John Constantine knows the cost of magic. During his youth, one of the first spells he cast caused a fire that led to the loss of his parents. Further experimentation with magic as a teenager transformed his first girlfriend into a ghost-eating monster. John then dedicated himself to learning everything he could from the greatest magicians, in the hopes that he would never accidentally hurt another person he loved again.

While John eventually became one of the most powerful and knowledgeable magicians on Earth, his overconfidence can occasionally lead to mistakes, such as exorcisms going horribly wrong. Although John's career as a magician has featured many triumphs, including a stint with a magic-based Super Hero team named the Justice League Dark, he finds it hard to forget the mistakes he made in the past.

Openly bisexual, John has had relationships with men and women. But these relationships never last, as John is reluctant to get too close to anyone. While he knows the costs of magic, it is always someone else who pays the price.

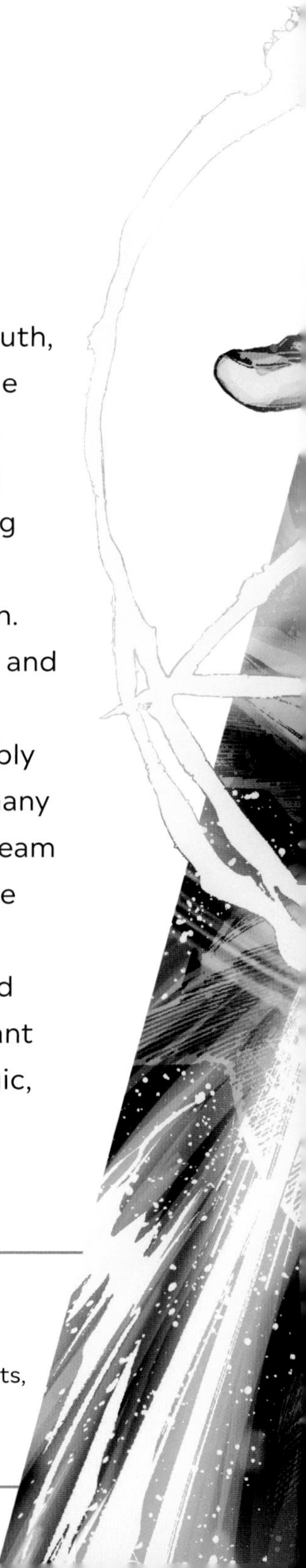

DATA FILE

First appearance: *Swamp Thing* (Vol. 2) #37 (1985)
Base: The House of Mystery
Likes: Bartenders that don't talk, getting lost, Zatanna
Dislikes: Uninvited guests, most angels, bicycles

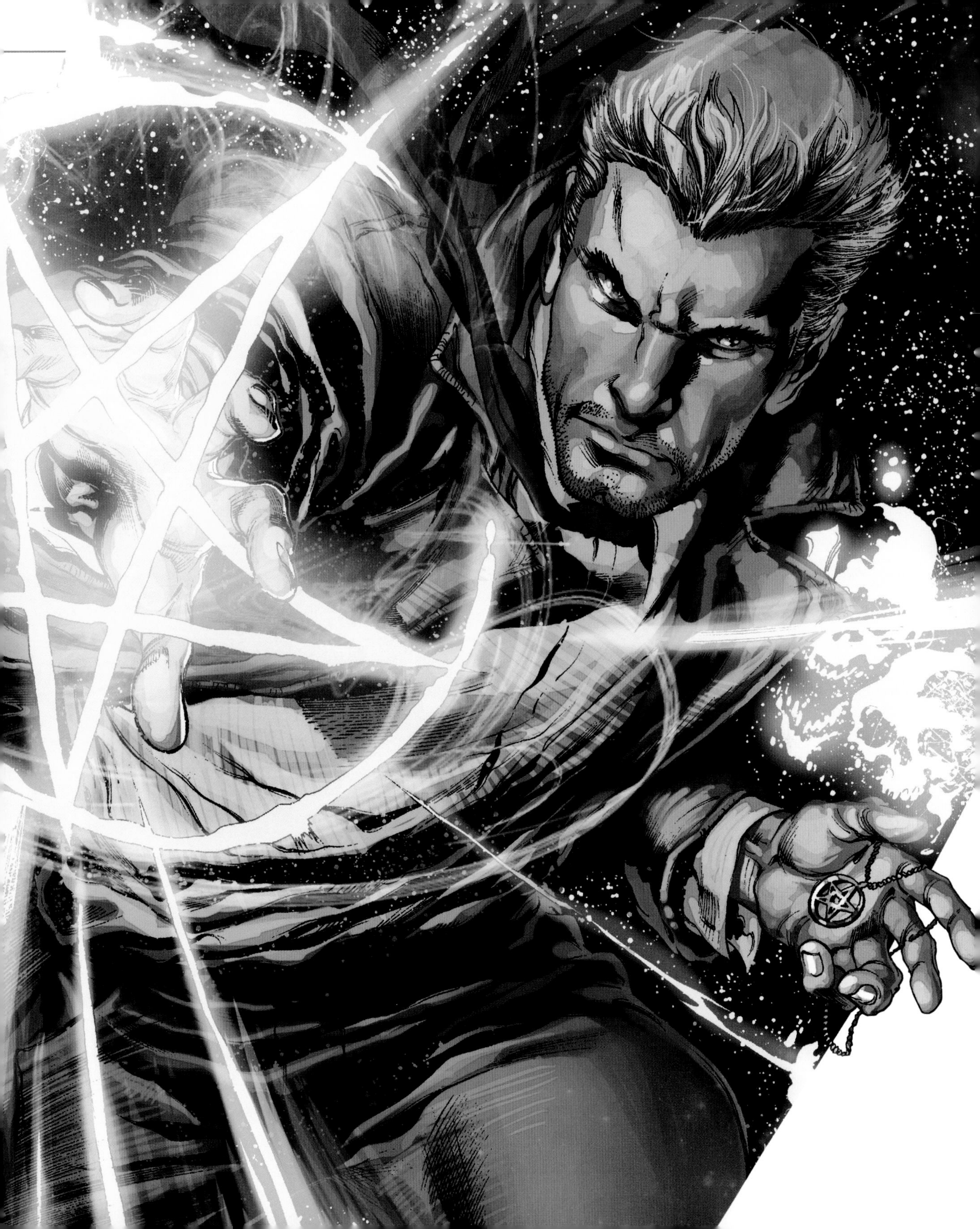

MAGGIE SAWYER

She/her

"The best we can hope for is to get out of this mess alive."

Experienced detective Margaret "Maggie" Sawyer was an essential part of the Metropolis Police Department's Special Crimes Unit, tasked with taking care of dangerous threats that would normally be handled by Superman. This role often put her in conflict *with* Superman, but the two eventually came to have a grudging respect for one another.

Maggie later moved to Gotham City to lead the Major Crimes Unit there, leaving her long-term girlfriend behind in Metropolis. Once again, Maggie's no-nonsense attitude and general distrust of masked vigilantes put her at odds with some of the officers under her command, such as Renee Montoya, as well as with Batman and Batwoman.

Maggie fell hard for Gotham City socialite Kate Kane, and after dancing together at a charity ball, they soon began dating. When Maggie discovered that Kate was Batwoman, her attitude toward Super Heroes began to change. Kate later proposed to Maggie, but ultimately got cold feet, and the wedding never happened. It was a tough situation to get through, but Maggie soldiered on, just like she always does.

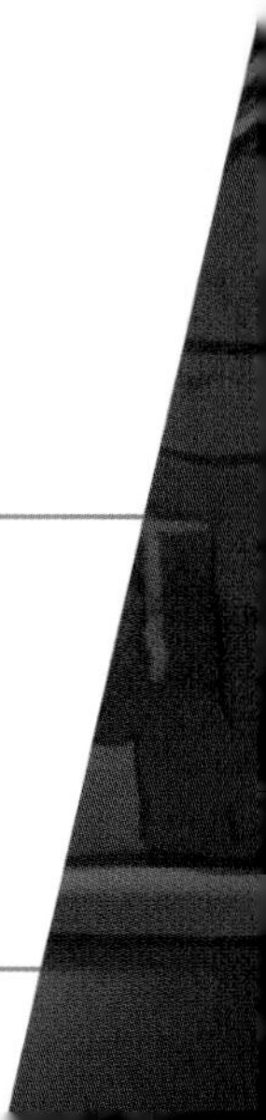

DATA FILE

First appearance: *Superman* (Vol. 2) #4 (1987)

Allies: Batwoman (Kate Kane), Superman (Clark Kent), Renee Montoya

Likes: Freshly cut hair, a well-organized filing system

Dislikes: Blackmail, empty files, socks with holes

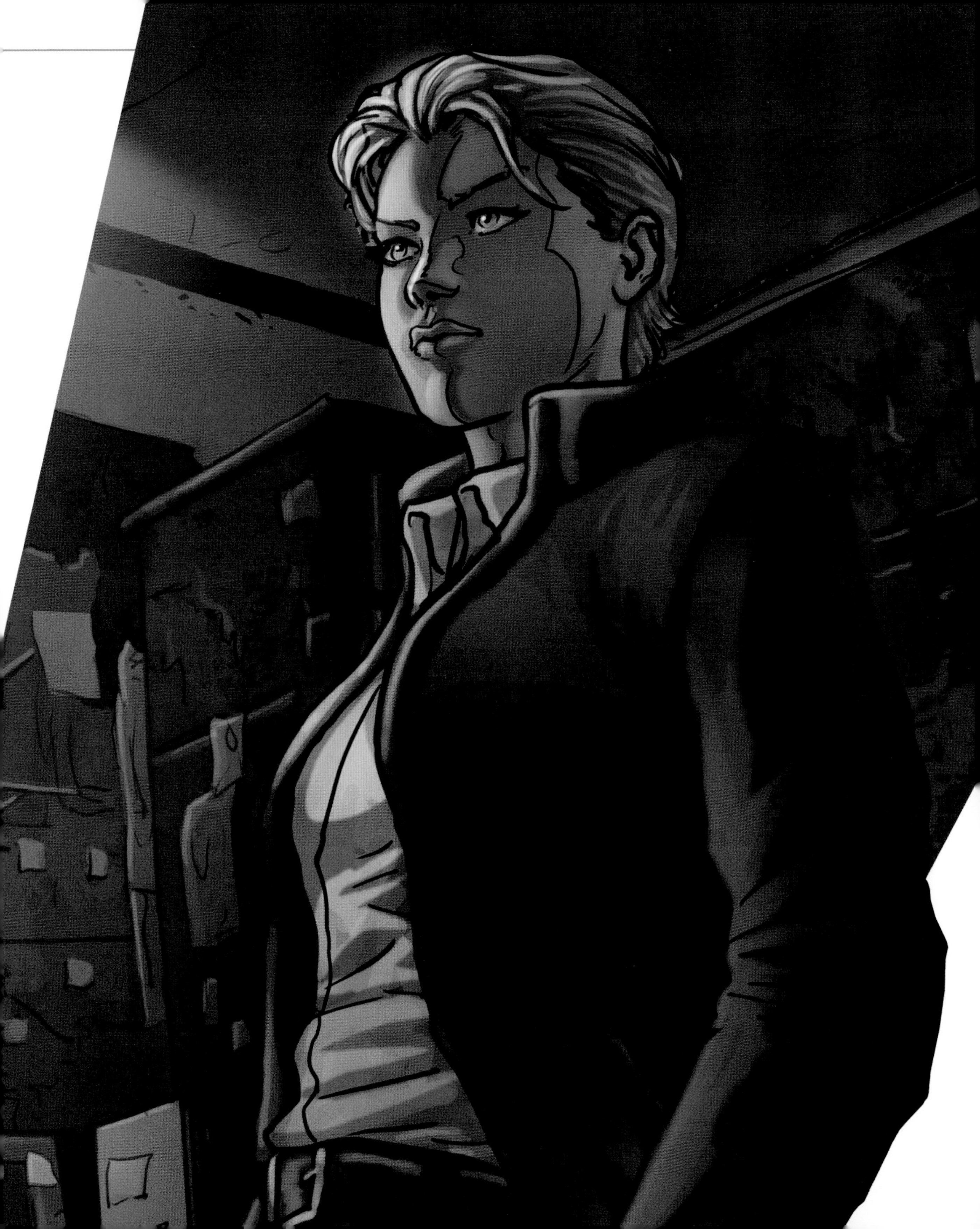

MIDNIGHTER

He/him

"This is our story. And in our story, we don't die in the end."

Midnighter's past is a mystery—even to himself. All he knows is that he was an agent of the Gardener, a scientist who carried out several dangerous experiments on a space station named the God Garden.

To try and fit in with society, Midnighter took the name Lucas Trent and worked as a professional soldier. Midnighter possesses superhuman strength, speed, and healing abilities, as well as a backup heart. But the most extraordinary tool in his arsenal is the combat computer implanted in his brain, which allows him to see every possible outcome of a battle before it happens. In a world of martial arts masters and career costumed brawlers, Midnighter may be the best fighter there is.

While working as a soldier, Midnighter noticed the powerful vigilante Apollo, admiring his methods and drive. When the two began working side by side, a romantic relationship developed between them, and they eventually married. Together, they became key members of Super Hero teams like Stormwatch and The Authority, fighting greater threats than they could ever conquer alone.

DATA FILE

First appearance: *Stormwatch* (Vol. 2) #4 (1998)
Allies: Apollo, Nightwing, Extraño
Likes: Weaponry, one-liners, stealing the covers
Dislikes: All of Apollo's favorite romance movies, without exception

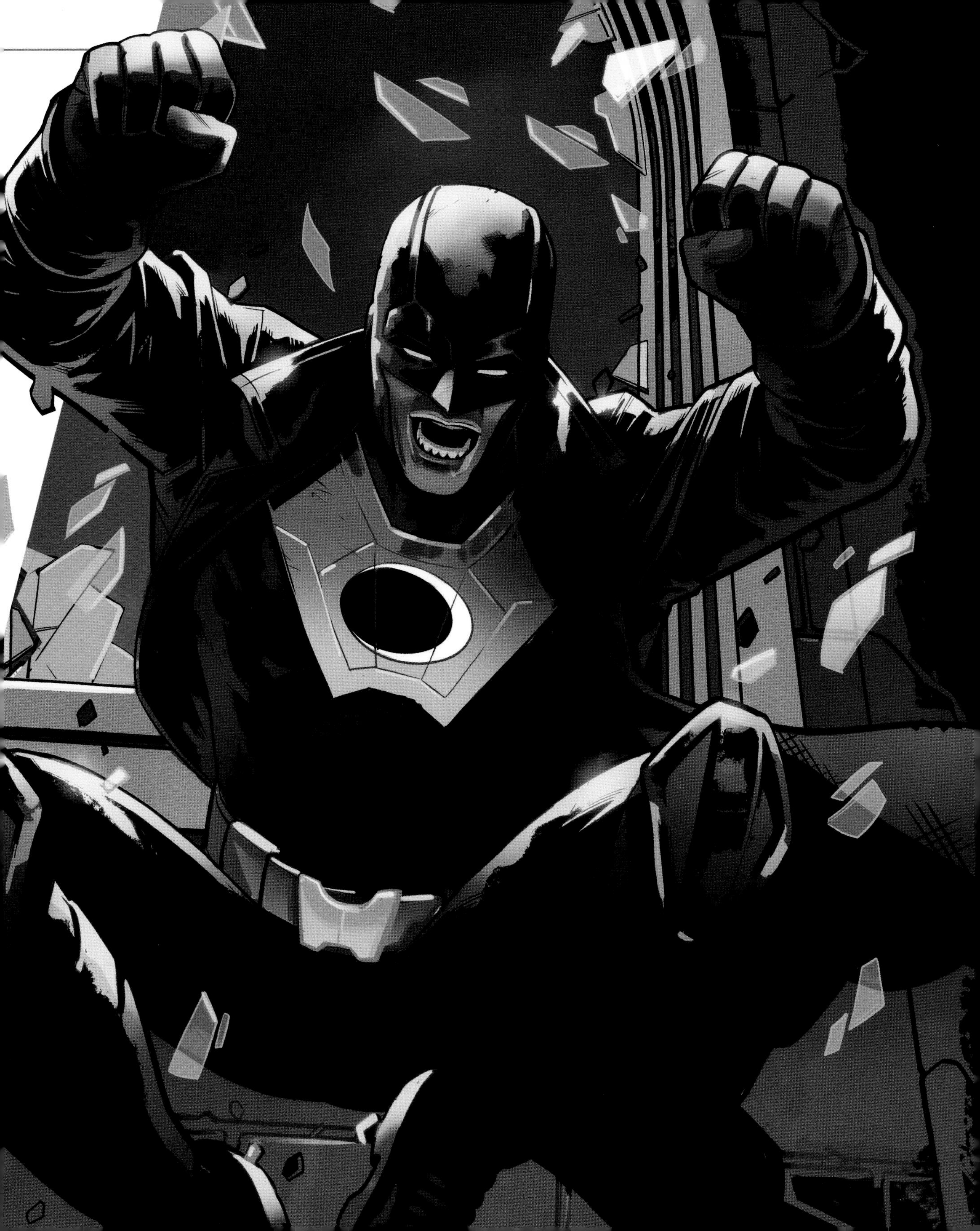

NUBIA

She/her

"I believe it is one's **actions**, not their **words**, that hold their **truth.**"

The Amazon warrior Nubia has always represented the highest ideals of honor and bravery. She was reborn from the Well of Souls on Themyscira at the same time that Wonder Woman was given life by the gods, and the two have lived as sisters ever since. For many years, Nubia was the guardian of Doom's Doorway, a gateway in the caves of Themyscira leading to the realm of Hades. It was her duty to ensure that any monsters that escaped through the Doorway were swiftly captured.

When Queen Hippolyta offered a test to decide who should be her successor, only Nubia stepped forward and conquered it, proving herself worthy of the crown. As Queen of the Amazons, Nubia rules with a focus on the bonds of community and unity between her Amazonian sisters—and no bond is stronger than Nubia's relationship with Io, the most gifted weaponsmith in Themyscira. Whenever the demands of ruling become too hard to bear, Nubia can be found in the soft embrace of Io's arms.

DATA FILE

First appearance: *Wonder Woman* (Vol. 1) #204 (1973)
Base: Themyscira
Allies: Hippolyta, Io, Wonder Woman

Likes: Helping women in need, cooking, pro wrestling

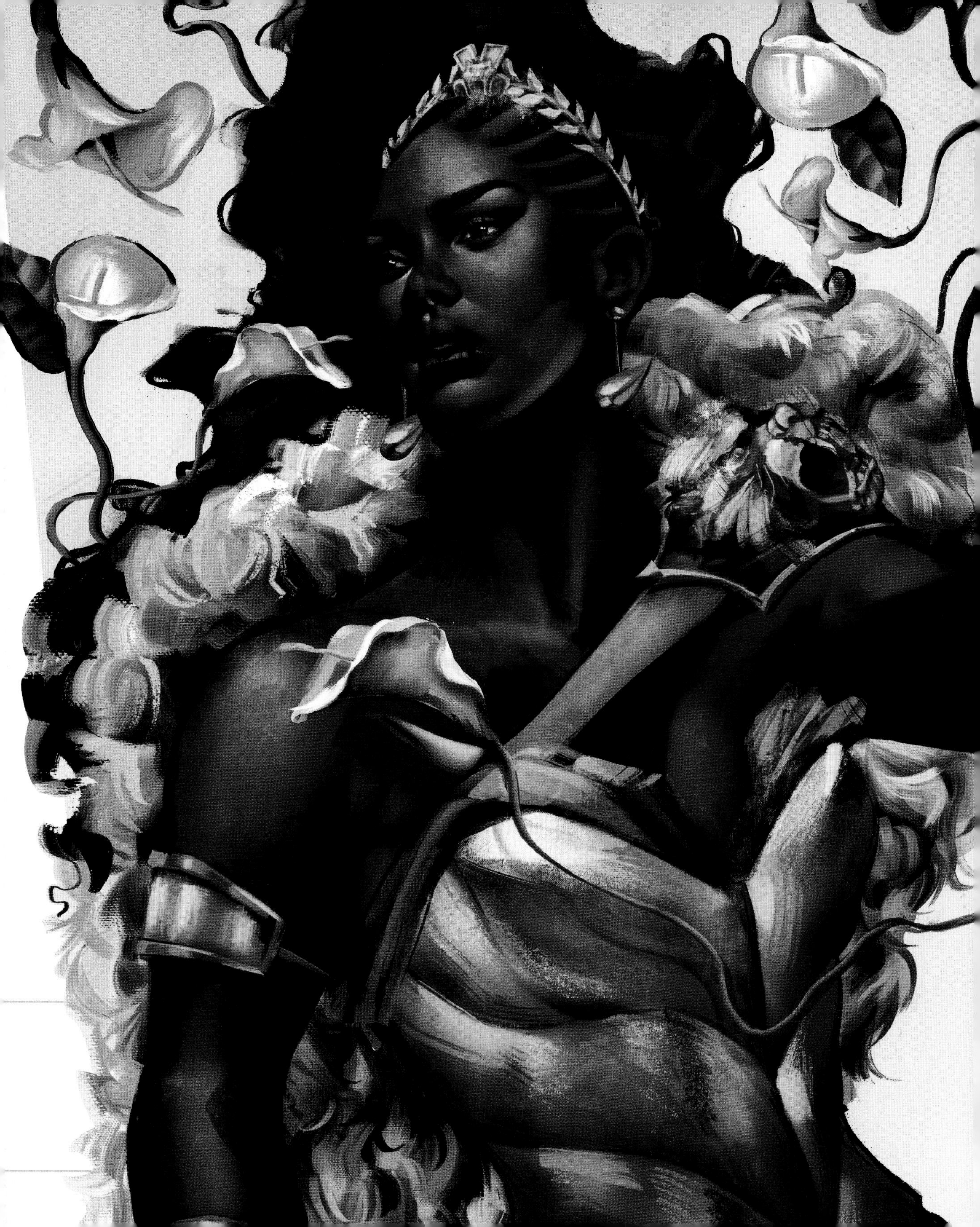

OBSIDIAN

He/him

"Getting 'political?' Do you mean, existing?"

Todd Rice always lived in the shadow of his father, Alan Scott—the Green Lantern. As a result of his father's many battles with Super-Villains in the Shadowland—a realm of pure dark energy—Todd was born with a connection to that mystical world, and was able to manipulate the darkness the same way his father was able to manipulate light.

Inspired by Alan, Todd took on the name Obsidian and began a successful career as a Super Hero, first as a founding member of Infinity, Inc., followed by a brief stint in the Justice League. But when the powers that allowed him to do so much good began to overwhelm him, he turned into a villain, threatening his friends and loved ones. In the end, Alan was the only one who was able to bring back the hero everyone knew.

Following this terrifying experience, Todd reevaluated his life and what was important, and he came out as a gay man. Since then, he has fallen in love with a lawyer named Damon Matthews. When the couple met Todd's father for a meal, Alan revealed his son's confidence inspired him to come out as a gay man, too.

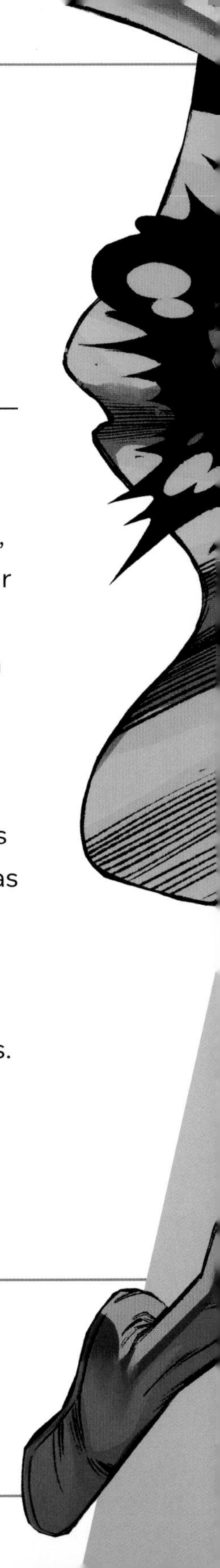

DATA FILE

First appearance: *All-Star Squadron* (Vol. 1) #25 (1983)
Allies: Alan Scott, Jade, Fury
Likes: Stephen Sondheim, queer-owned venues
Dislikes: Tanning beds, high noon

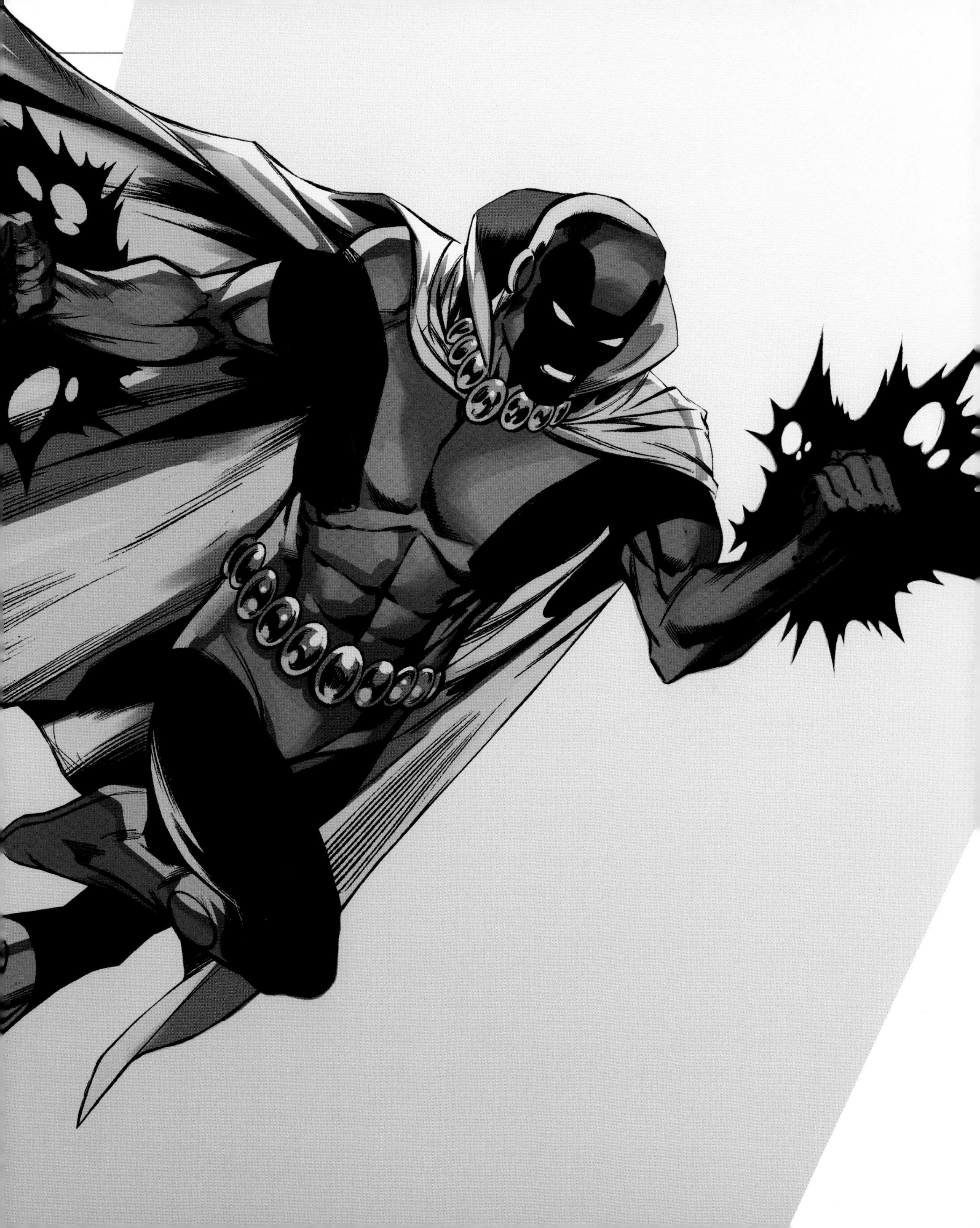

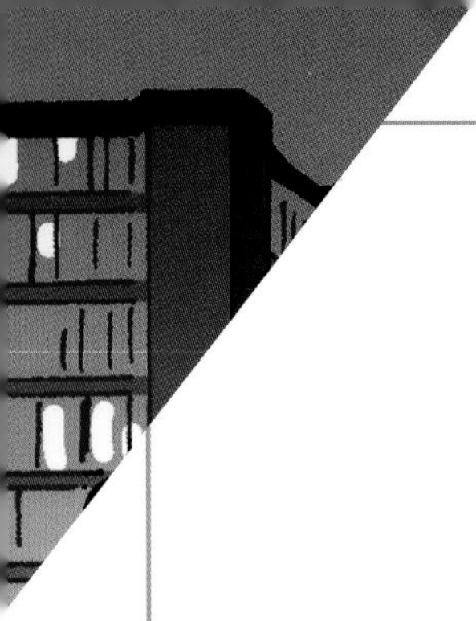

THE PIED PIPER

He/him

"Central City needs me.

It needs The Pied Piper."

When Hartley Rathaway was born deaf, his wealthy parents poured their resources into expensive surgeries that resulted in Hartley becoming able to hear—at which point he became fascinated with music and sound. As an adult, Hartley grew bored of his rich lifestyle and rebelled by becoming a costumed criminal known as The Pied Piper—complete with his own flute that could hypnotize others into doing whatever he wanted.

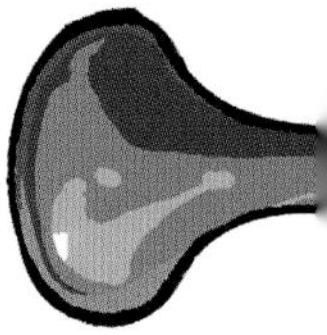

Hartley frequently clashed with Barry Allen, The Flash, and joined a team of criminals named The Rogues. But after Barry died saving the Multiverse, Hartley decided to change his tune and retire from crime, becoming a vigilante hero instead. He became good friends with Barry's successor to The Flash mantle, Wally West, and came out as gay.

Since then, Hartley has had several boyfriends and started working as a conductor at the Central City Symphony. Hartley may have hung up his Pied Piper costume, but he continues to live his life loudly and proudly!

DATA FILE

First appearance: *Flash* (Vol. 1) #106 (1959)
Base: Central City
Abilities: Hypnosis, sound manipulation, sonic blasts
Likes: Men in uniform, wind instruments, rats

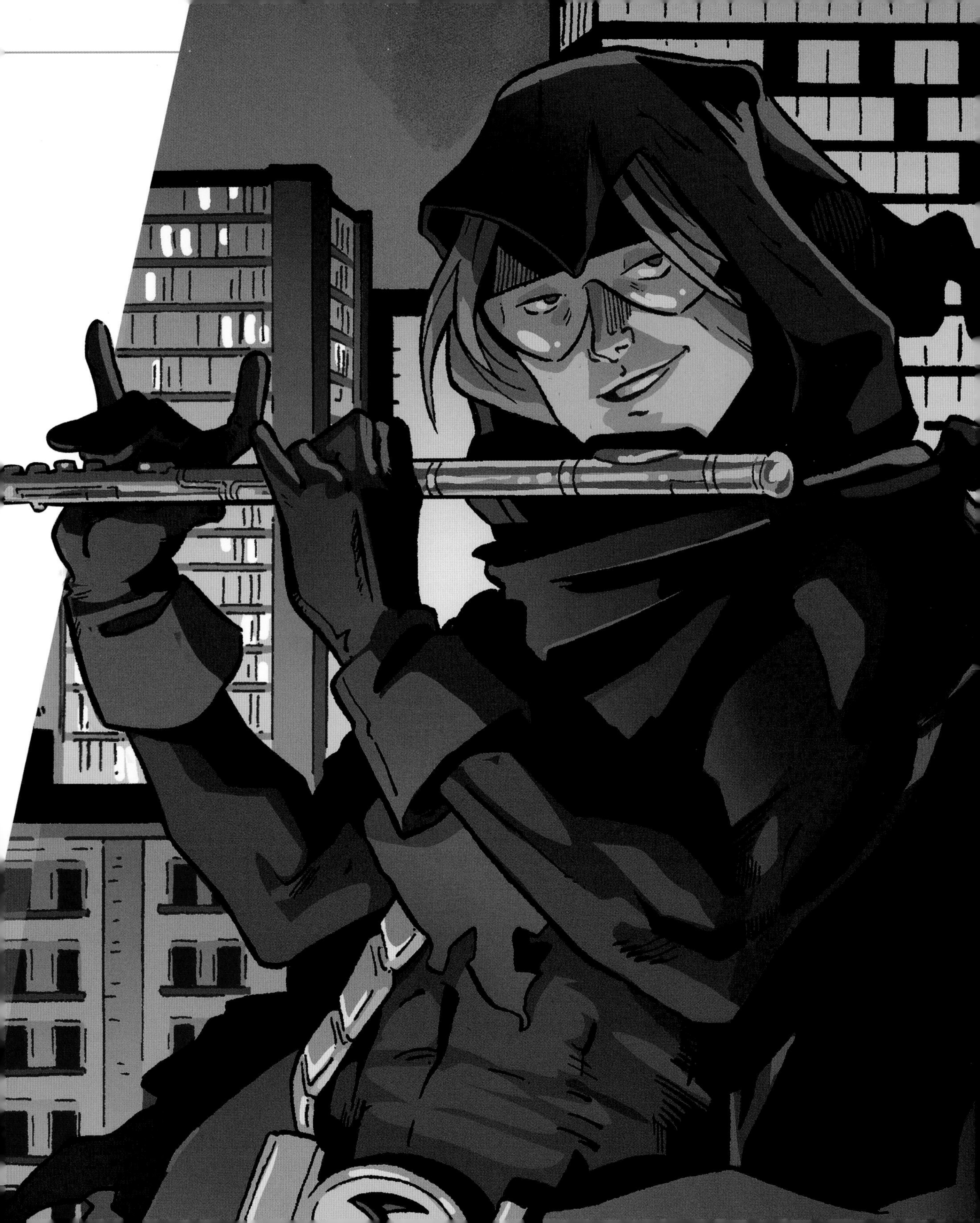

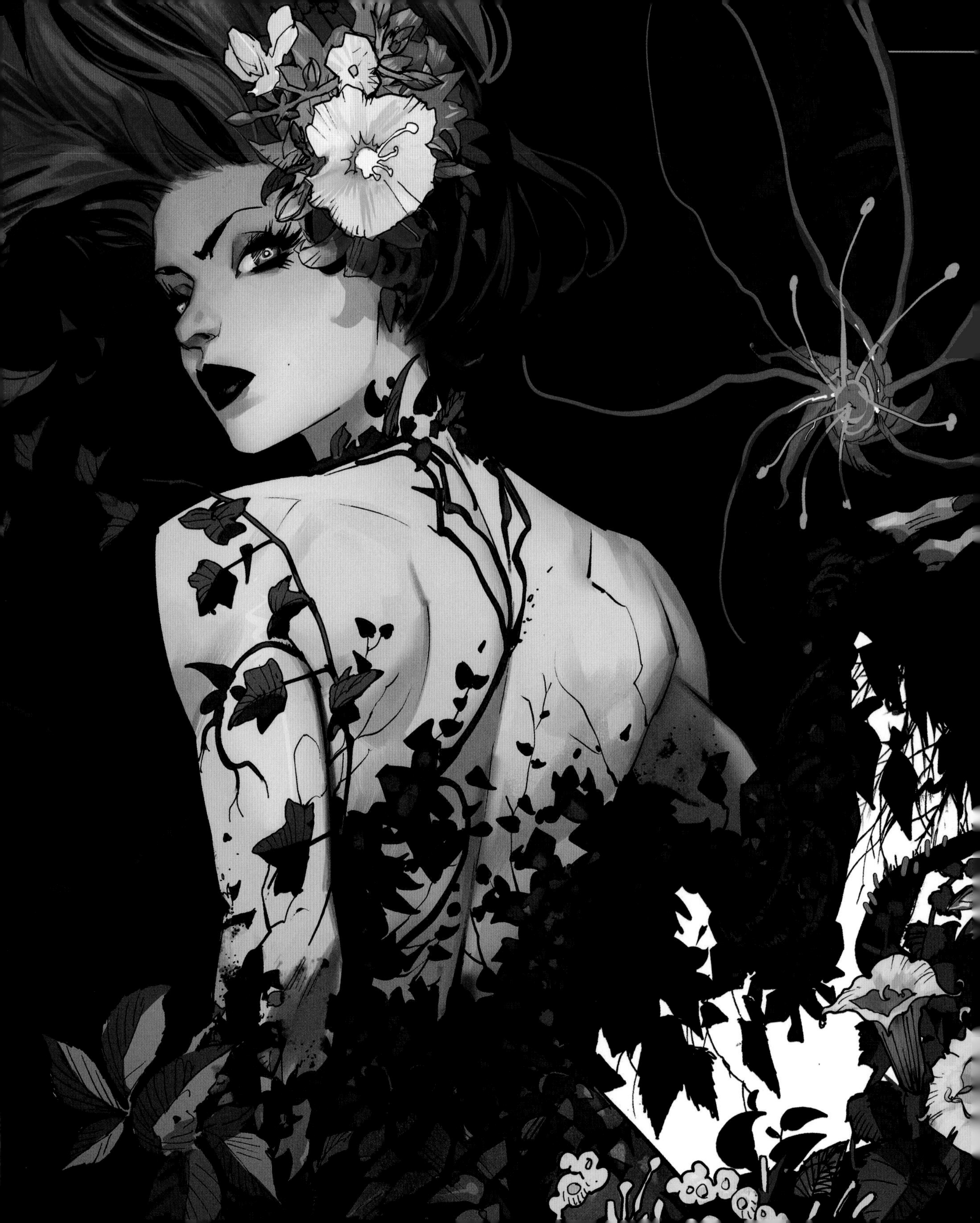

POISON IVY

She/her

"I am the **Queen** of the May, **crowned** in leaves, and blossom, and **thorns.**"

Dedicated environmentalist and genius botanist Pamela Isley has always known that you can't have a thriving garden without pruning a few weeds. With her poison kiss and supernatural control over plant life, Pamela made a career out of taking down those who would harm the planet for personal gain. Dubbing herself "Poison Ivy," she became one of the most noteworthy Super-Villains in Batman's Rogues Gallery.

While Ivy often faked admiration and affection to get what she wanted, her friendship with fellow Gotham City Siren Harley Quinn later blossomed into a sincere love. While their relationship has never been perfect, the couple care deeply for each other, and Harley's mischievous nature has helped Ivy learn to drop her guard and enjoy herself once in a while.

While Harley is still figuring out where she falls on the scale of good and evil, Ivy has redoubled her efforts to destroy anyone who dares to damage the environment. In Ivy's eyes, the whole world is her garden, and she has much to tend to.

DATA FILE
First appearance: *Batman* (Vol. 1) #181 (1966)
Allies: Harley Quinn, Catwoman

Likes: Plants. That's pretty much it—bar Harley
Dislikes: People

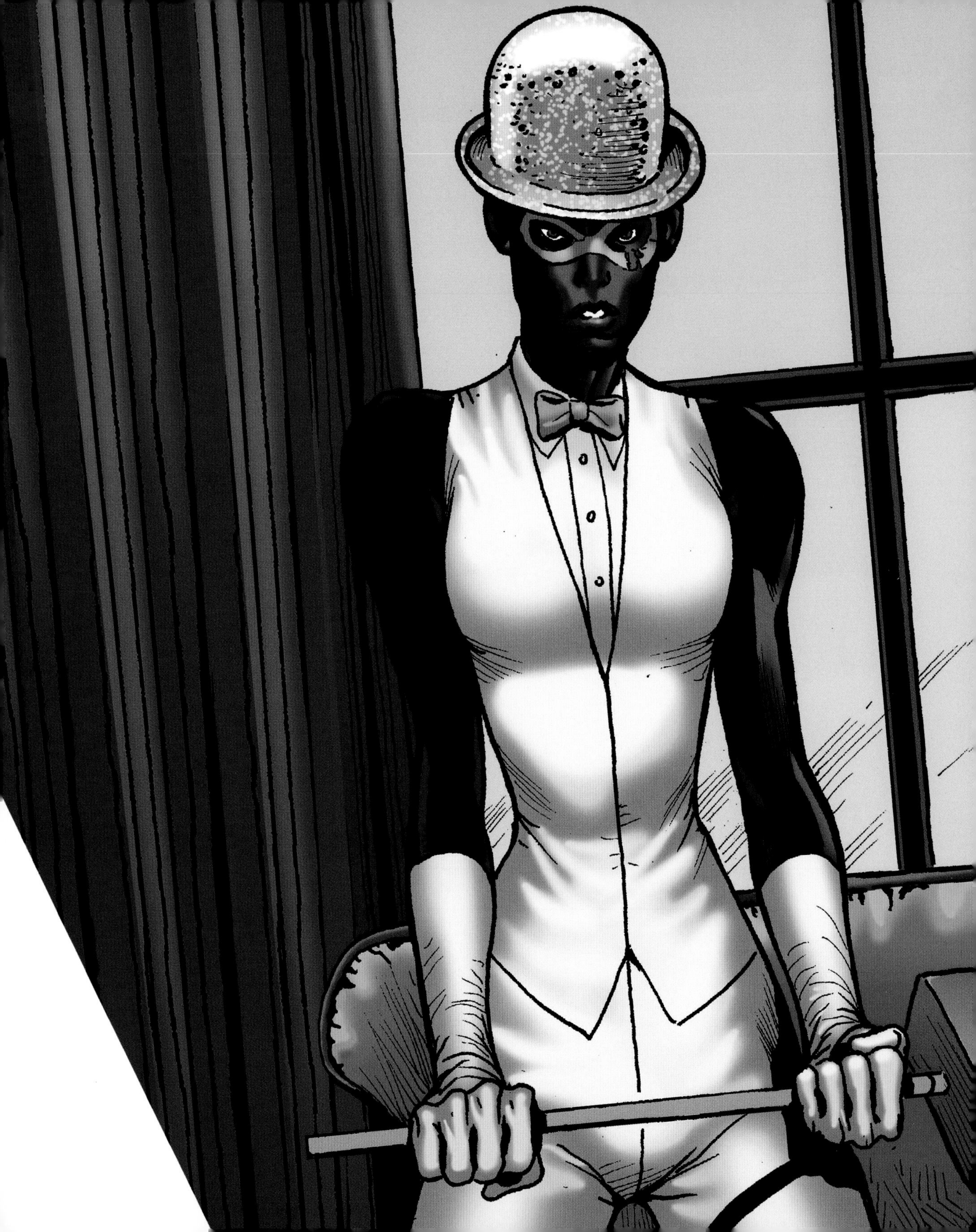

PORCELAIN

They/them

"If there's anything I know... it's **makeovers!**"

Porcelain may be one of the most mysterious residents of Gotham City. This member of the villainous group Secret Six possesses the dangerous ability to render any substance brittle just by touching it, making it fragile enough to shatter like glass.

Porcelain always plays their cards close to their chest and has revealed very little about themself—even to their teammates. Only a few things are known for certain: they are a criminal of exceptional skill and reputation; they are a remarkable fighter and can make good use of a sledgehammer; they are bisexual and genderfluid. When they feel like a girl, they use the name Kani, and when they don't, they use the name Kevin. When they feel like crime, they use the name Porcelain.

As someone with the power to make things crack and crumble if they push too hard, it's no surprise that Porcelain is reluctant to get too close to others. They were in a relationship with one of their Secret Six teammates, Catman, but as neither villain is known for showing their true emotions, how they really felt about each other is up for debate!

DATA FILE

First appearance: *Secret Six* (Vol. 4) #1 (2015)
Allies: Catman, Scandal Savage
Likes: Crop tops, the sound of glass cracking, cats
Dislikes: Waiting in line, being told what to do, liars

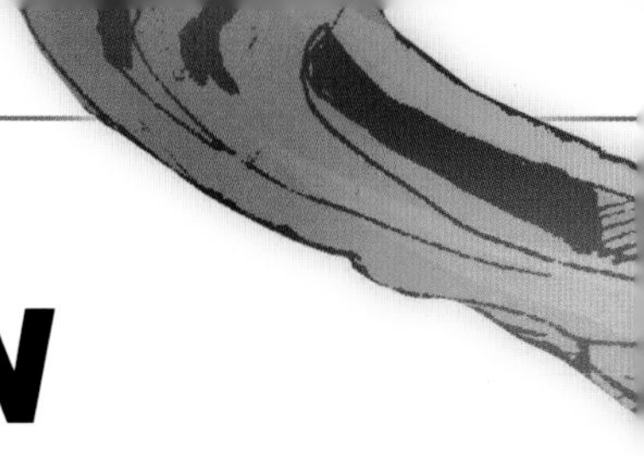

THE QUESTION
(RENEE MONTOYA)

She/her

"You have to know the question to find the answer."

Renee Montoya was always looking for answers. She began her career as a detective with the Gotham City Police Department, but the longer she worked with the police, the more she became convinced that she was doing more harm than good. When Renee realized that the department was full of people who could not be trusted, she knew she would find no answers there.

After quitting the force, Renee was approached by Vic Sage, a faceless vigilante known as The Question. He needed her help to find answers of his own, and the two detectives worked together to investigate the dark dealings of the sinister Cult of Crime. Although the pair made a strong team, Vic soon succumbed to a serious illness, leaving Renee to take on his faceless mask and become The Question in his place.

Since then, Renee has clashed with her old boss, Maggie Sawyer, and teamed up with her old girlfriend Kate Kane in her Super Hero guise as Batwoman. In spite of fighting a daily battle against her own demons, Renee is determined to make the world a better place. As The Question, Renee may finally have a way to find the answers she was searching for.

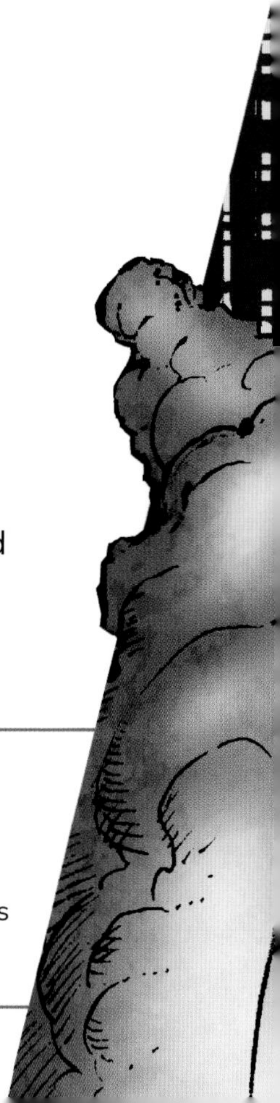

DATA FILE

First appearance: *Batman* (Vol. 1) #475 (1992)
Allies: The Question (Vic Sage), Maggie Sawyer, Batwoman (Kate Kane)
Likes: Arepas, red string, clean sheets
Dislikes: Billboards, girlfriends stealing her clothes

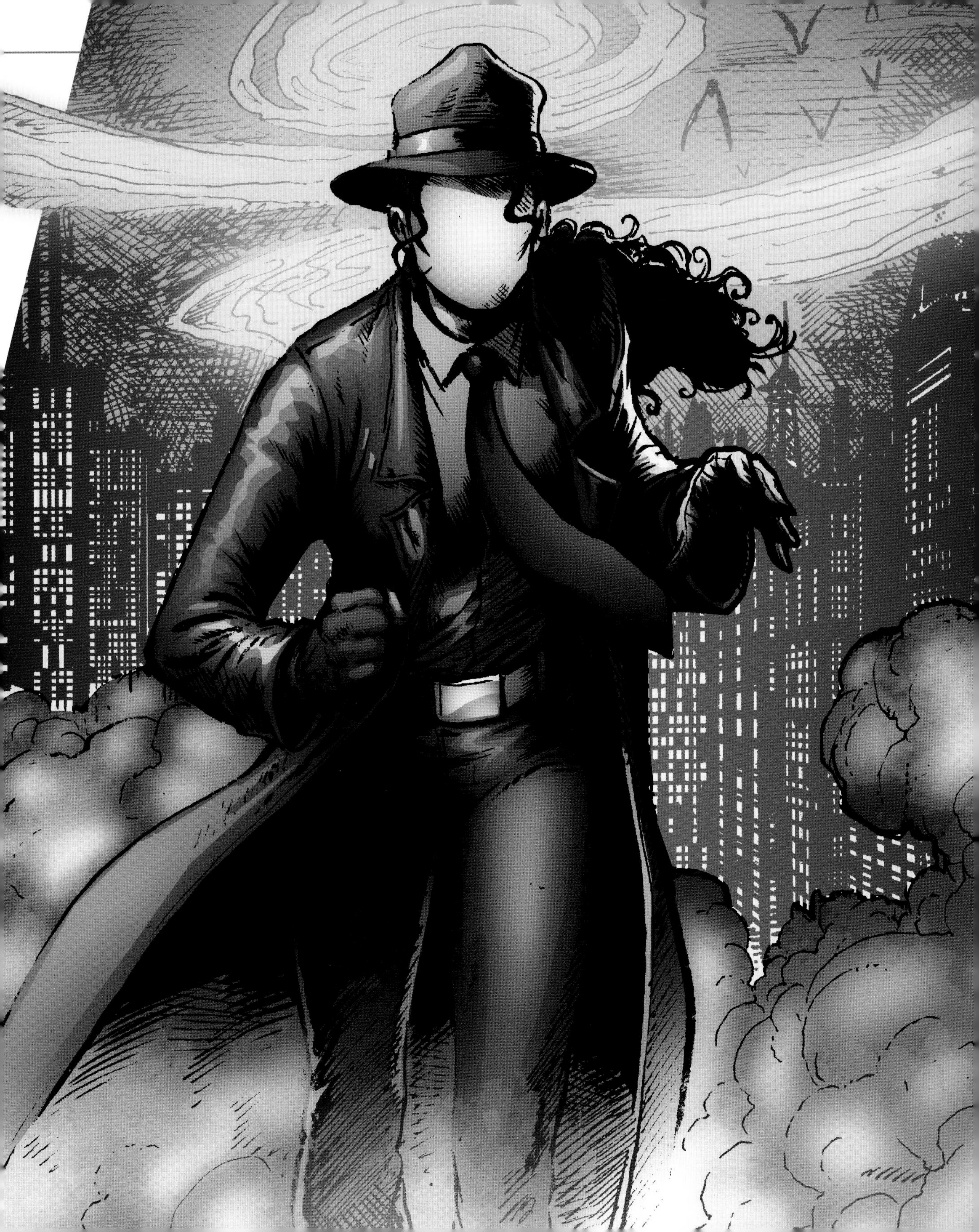

THE RAY
(RAY TERRILL)
He/him

> "Whatever comes next, for the **first** time, I'm ready... because the future looks **bright.**"

Growing up, Raymond "Ray" Terrill was kept in the dark—literally. His mother knew he had the ability to absorb and manipulate light and feared he'd accidentally hurt others with his powers, so she said he was fatally allergic to light to keep him indoors. Ray eventually grew tired of staying in his own home, and when he was 18, he ran away. Though he enjoyed a few hours of freedom, soon Ray lost control of his powers and nearly harmed a stranger, as his mother always feared. Ashamed with himself, Ray used his powers to turn himself invisible and stopped interacting with others.

But when a childhood friend became the target of a violent attack, Ray realized that he could not hide from the injustices around him forever and took on a Super Hero identity, the Ray. The Ray became a beacon to those around him, and soon joined the Justice League of America.

An openly gay man, Ray began a relationship with his Justice League teammate Xenos. Like Ray, Xenos had a difficult childhood, and every day the two men work together to move on from their pasts toward a brighter future.

DATA FILE

First appearance: *Justice League of America: The Ray Rebirth* #1 (2017)
Base: Vanity, Oregon

Likes: Old movies, flying, popcorn with tons of butter
Dislikes: Darkness, his mother

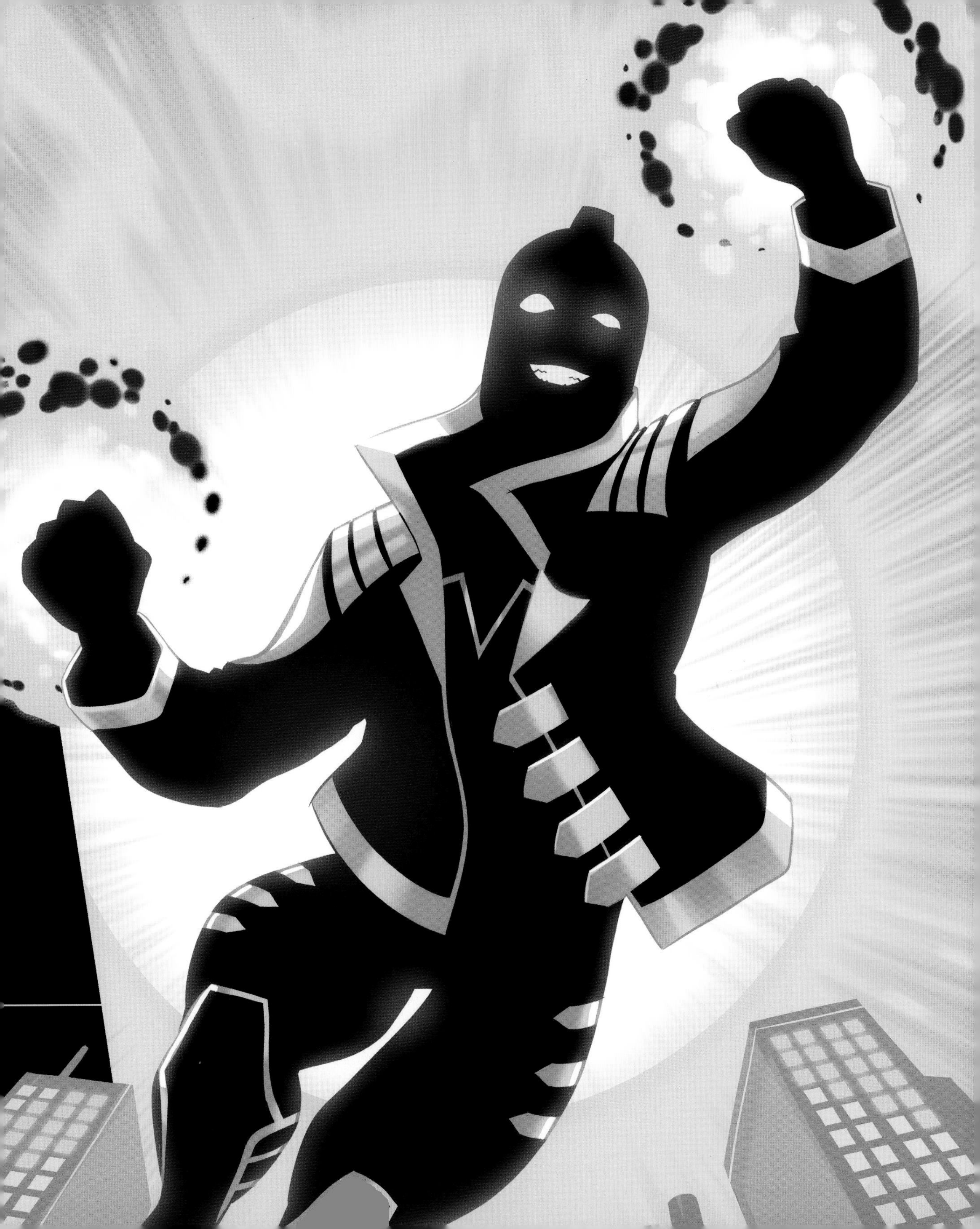

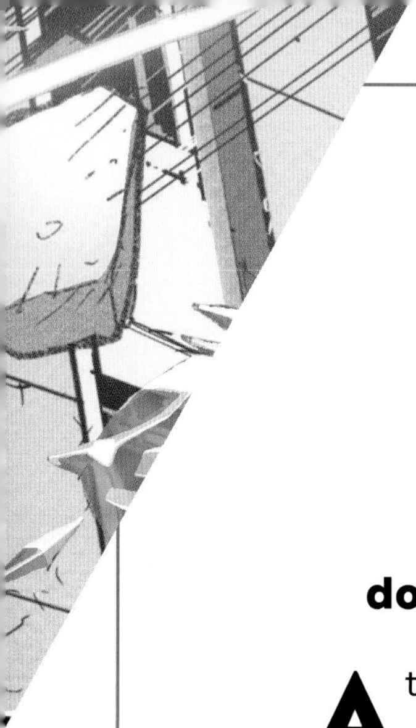

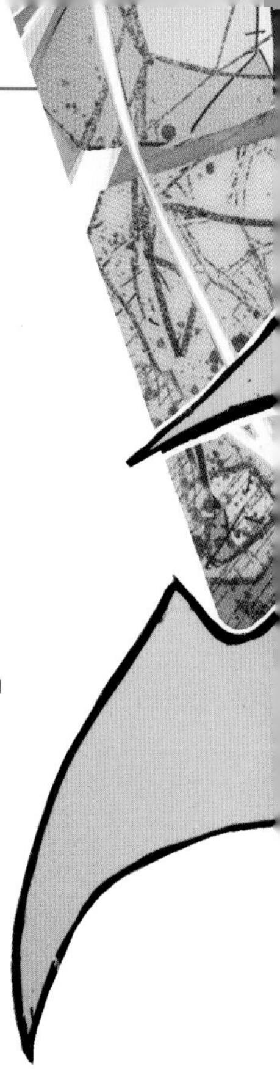

ROBIN
(TIM DRAKE)

He/him

"This is what happens when you give a sixteen-year-old genius who doesn't sleep an unlimited budget."

At a young age, Tim Drake figured out that Batman and Robin were Bruce Wayne and Dick Grayson respectively, and closely followed their adventures. After the death of Jason Todd, the second Robin, Tim helped Batman in a battle against the Super-Villain Two-Face. Tim's courage and intelligence convinced Batman, reluctantly, to train him.

As Robin, Tim Drake defined himself as much more than a sidekick. He'd go on frequent solo missions and lead Super Hero teams Young Justice and the Teen Titans. When Bruce Wayne's son, Damian Wayne, took on the Robin mantle, Tim flew from the Batcave to be his own hero, taking on the heroic identity Red Robin, and, for a short period, Drake.

Tim may be a master detective who has earned the respect of international criminal mastermind Rā's al Ghūl, but when it comes to his own heart, he barely has a clue! His on-again, off-again romance with fellow vigilante Stephanie Brown, a.k.a. Batgirl, was full of missteps, something Tim is hoping to avoid with his first boyfriend, Bernard Dowd.

DATA FILE

First appearance: *Batman* (Vol. 1) #436 (1989)
Aliases: Robin, Red Robin, Drake, Savior, Alvin Draper, Iggy Pollaky
Likes: Computers, Sherlock Holmes movies, playing "Warlocks & Warriors" RPG
Dislikes: Sleep, being wrong, other people being Robin

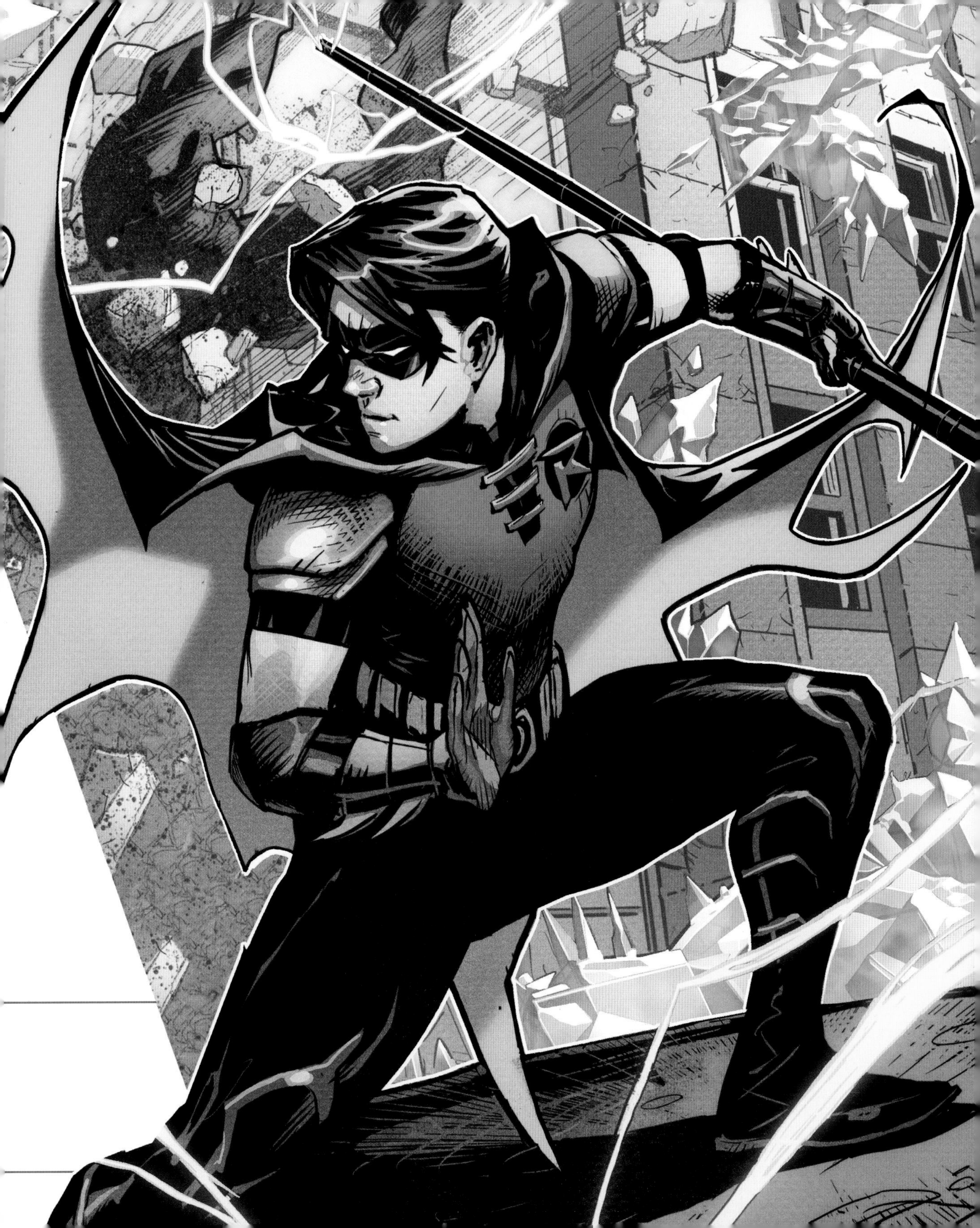

SARAH RAINMAKER

She/her

"I have a typhoon in one hand and a tsunami in the other. And you want to threaten me?"

Sarah Rainmaker was always comfortable being on the outside. A teenage girl of Apache heritage, Sarah grew up on the San Carlos Reservation in Arizona, never really feeling like she fit in. She had no idea how to act upon her romantic feelings toward other girls, preferring to keep things bottled up inside.

Everything changed for Sarah when a government agency experimented on her and four other teenagers in the hope that their invasive procedures would activate superpowers within their captives. They referred to the group as Gen 13. When Sarah and her new friends broke free, she realized she had found a connection she'd never had with other people. This bond led to Sarah coming out as a lesbian to the group—something she'd never told anyone before.

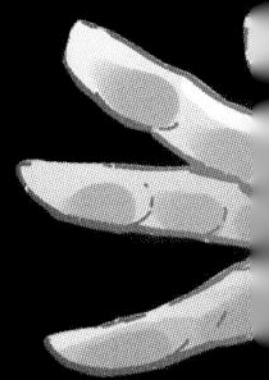

During her time with Gen 13, Sarah discovered she has the amazing power to control weather. Sarah can summon rain or lightning with just her thoughts and uses wind currents to fly from one mission to the next. These abilities became invaluable when she later joined Super Hero group The Movement.

DATA FILE

First appearance: *Gen 13* (Vol. 1) [illegible]

Likes: Feminism, popcorn, lattes

Dislikes: Super Hero codenames

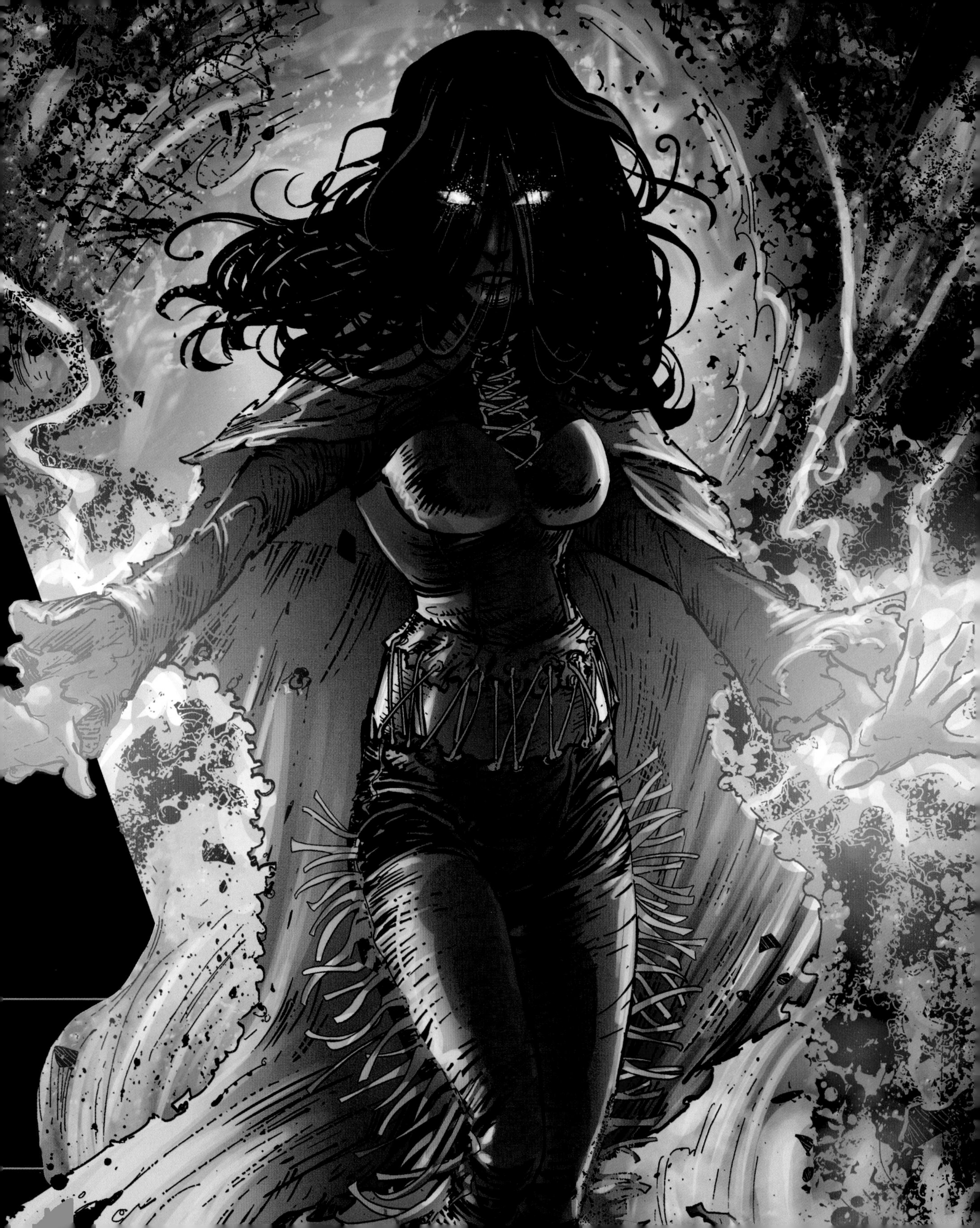

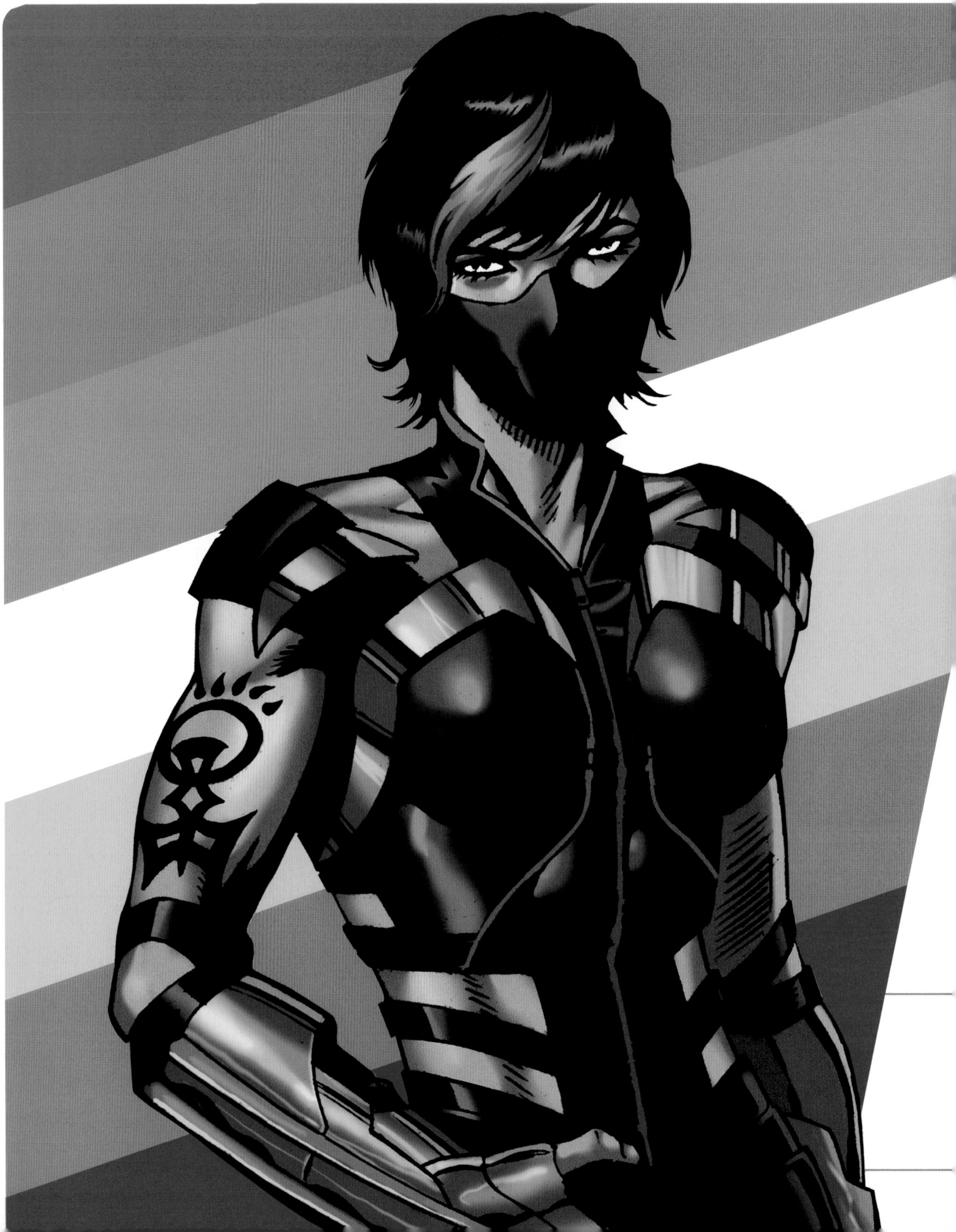

SCANDAL SAVAGE

She/her

"I wonder how you might feel, father, if someone were to control your life, for even a moment. Stings a bit, doesn't it?"

As a daughter of the immortal Vandal Savage, every moment of Scandal Savage's life was controlled in an attempt to create the perfect heir. But Scandal had no interest in being part of her father's legacy and eventually managed to escape. Free from her father's clutches, Scandal made a name for herself as a soldier for hire and assembled a team of villains who would come to be known as the Secret Six.

Scandal was never shy about being a lesbian, which was another major source of conflict between her and her father. She began a relationship with another powerful villain, Knockout, but this came to a tragic end when Knockout was suddenly killed. Although Scandal was heartbroken, she eventually found comfort in the arms of another woman named Liana.

When the Secret Six later journeyed to Hell, Scandal rescued Knockout and brought her back to the land of the living. Scandal then went on to retire, swapping a life of villainy for a life of domestic happiness with both Liana and Knockout.

DATA FILE

First appearance: *Villains United* (Vol. 1) #1 (2005)
Allies: Catman, Porcelain, Knockout, Deadshot

Abilities: Hand-to-hand combat, accelerated healing
Dislikes: Dull blades, dressing rooms

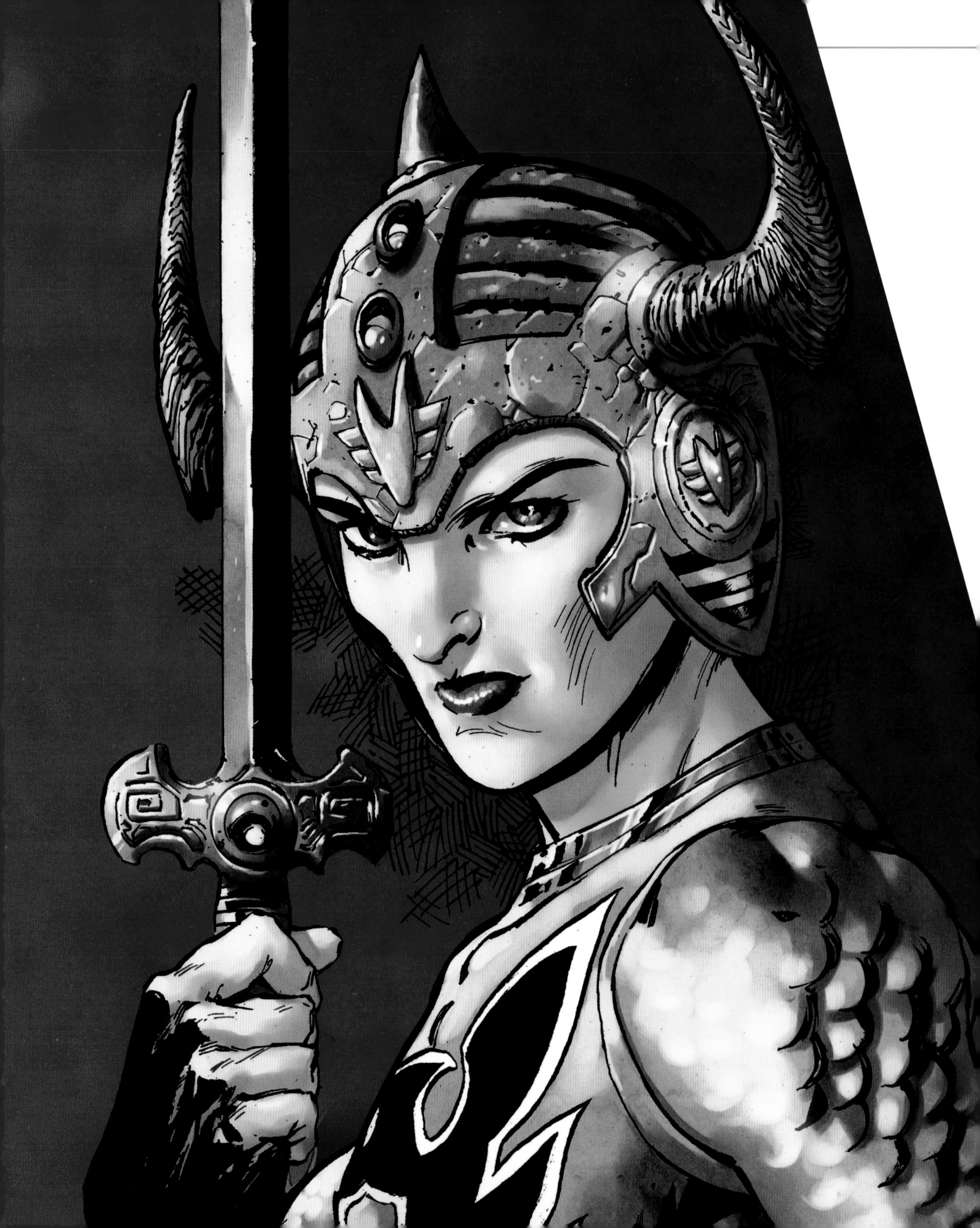

SHINING KNIGHT

They/them

"I was born this way. I've kept saying, whenever anyone asks, I'm not just a man or a woman, I'm both."

Hundreds of years ago, in the last great battle of Camelot, each of the noble Knights of the Round Table fell. It appeared that a mortally wounded young squire, Ystin, would be no different. But the wizard Merlin saw that Ystin possessed both a female and male nature, which gave the squire a valuable perspective. Merlin healed Ystin with a drink from the Holy Grail, granting them immortality. Ystin then traveled the world as a knight errant atop their winged horse Vanguard, becoming known as Shining Knight.

Many years later, Ystin teamed up with a collection of fighters and sorcerers called the Demon Knights. Among them was an exiled Amazon, Exoristos, with whom Ystin struck up an awkward flirtation. Though Exoristos was confused that Ystin was not only a woman, as she first assumed, but both a man AND a woman, she came to understand Ystin's true nature and the two began a heartfelt romance.

DATA FILE

First appearance: *Demon Knights* (Vol. 1) #1 (2011)
Bases: Camelot; Los Angeles

Likes: A sharp sword, a cool breeze on a summer's day
Dislikes: Fairies, modern fashion

STARMAN
(MIKAAL TOMAS)
He/him

> ## "Tragedy, it seems, is the gloomy tattered thing all of us metas are destined to drape around our shoulders."

A warrior from the planet Talok III, Mikaal Tomas was part of an invasion force tasked with conquering Earth during the 1970s. But once he saw that humans were capable of joy and beauty, he turned on his superiors. Before they could punish Mikaal, he escaped and fell to Earth, ready to defend it against all attackers—be they aliens or humans.

Mikaal was named "Starman" after the David Bowie song that was popular at the time, and he soon embraced the excitement of the disco age. Mikaal's sexuality can't be defined by human concepts, and cut off from his people, Mikaal struggled to find a connection with anyone on the dancefloor—until he met a man named Tony. Having finally found happiness, Mikaal decided to take a break from fighting villains so that he could spend time with his boyfriend. But when Tony tragically died, Mikaal felt he had no choice but to become a Super Hero once again, serving on the Justice League and returning to his role as Earth's protector.

DATA FILE
First appearance: *1st Issue Special* (Vol. 1) #12 (1976)
Base: Opal City

Likes: A solid V-neck shirt, a good party
Dislikes: Watergate salad, heavy metal music, being alone

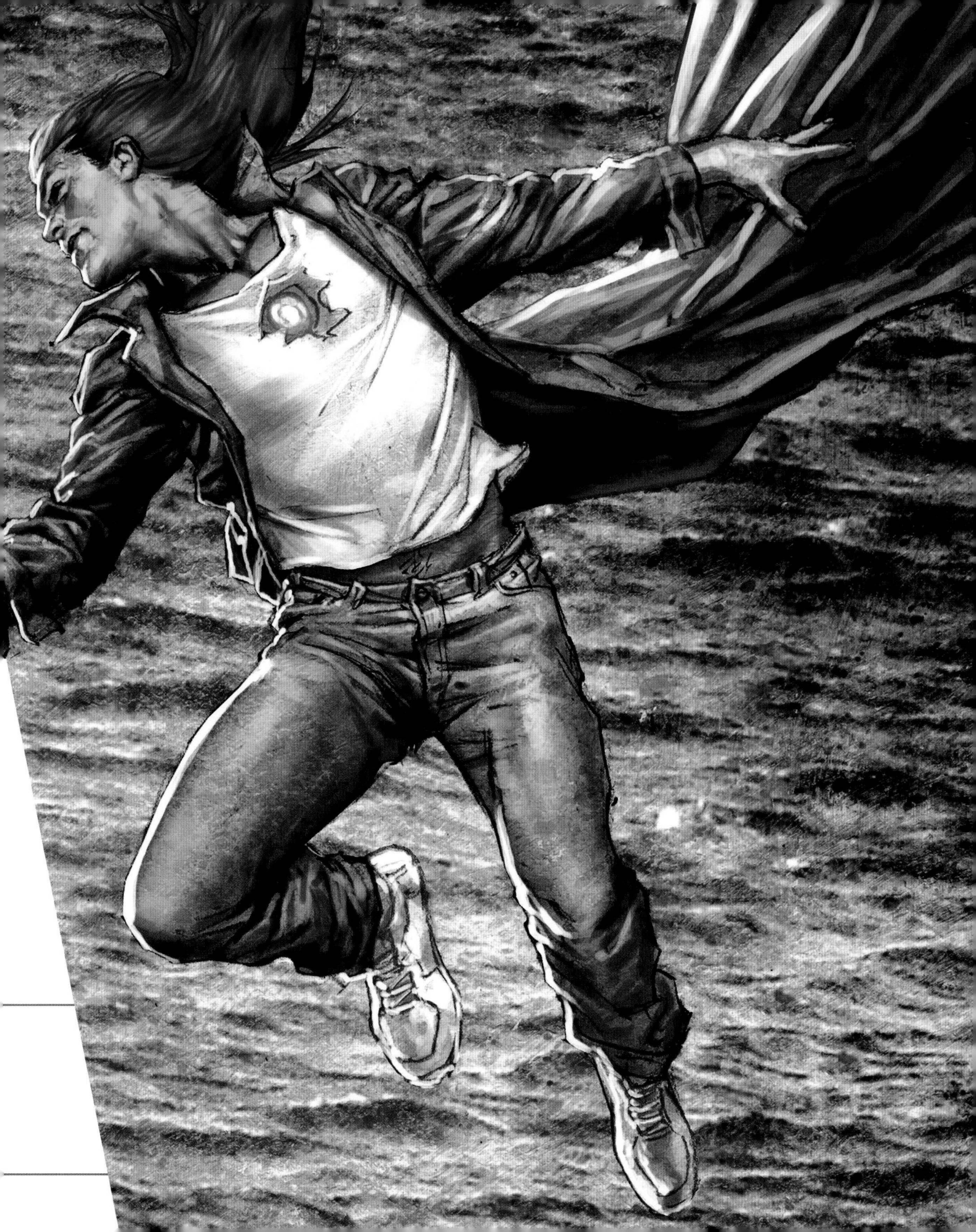

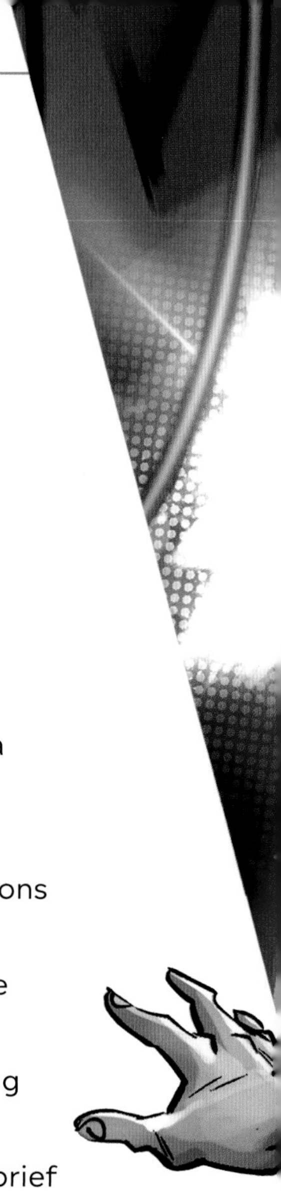

STEEL
(NATASHA IRONS)
She/her

"I'm the one with all the theories.
Welcome to the party."

Natasha Irons was never one to go slow. The genius niece of John Henry Irons, the first Super Hero named Steel, she graduated from high school early and whizzed through college. Natasha developed much of the technology in her uncle's superpowered armor and wasted no time crafting a suit for herself. Sharing the Steel mantle with John, Natasha flew into a life of heroics.

Natasha's flashy, technology-enhanced escapades soon caught the attention of other Super Heroes, leading to positions on many teams, including the Titans, the Authority, and even the Justice League. Always making upgrades to her armor, she now wields a morphing suit of semi-sentient chrome that gives her super-strength, allows her to fly, and offers a dazzling array of weaponry and sensor systems.

Although Natasha had many short-term girlfriends in her brief time at college, her longest relationship was with the young wizard Traci 13. But technology and magic don't always mix, and Natasha was forced to leave Traci behind as she continued, full speed ahead, on her heroic journey.

DATA FILE

First appearance: *Steel* (Vol. 2) #1 (1994)
Allies: Steel (John Henry Irons), Traci 13, Superman (Clark Kent), Midnighter, Apollo
Likes: A clean weld, overalls, bulldogs
Dislikes: Hypocrites, debris, forgetting to take her ADHD meds

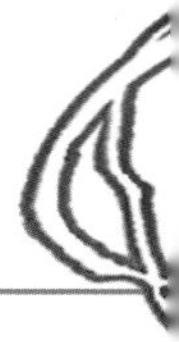

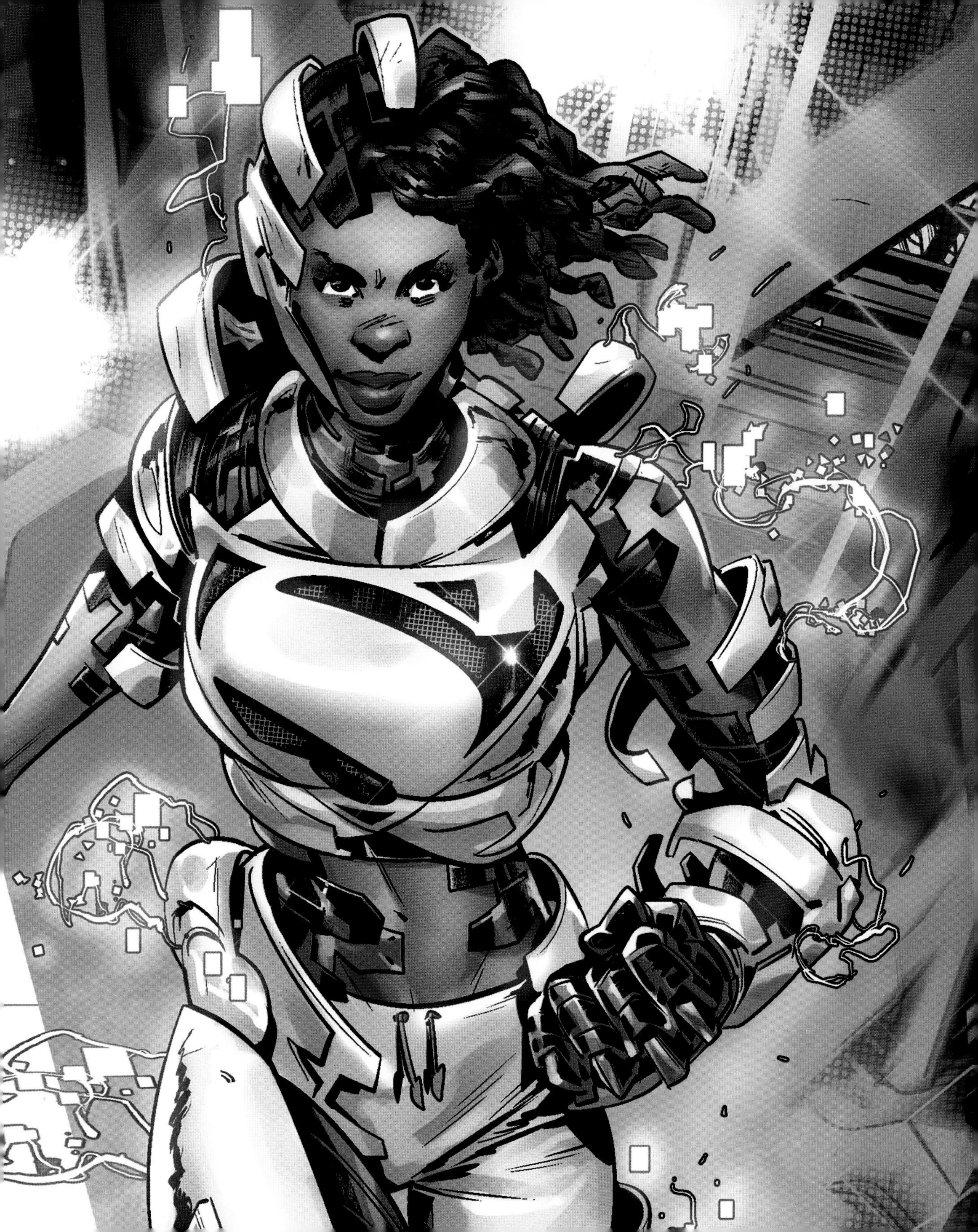

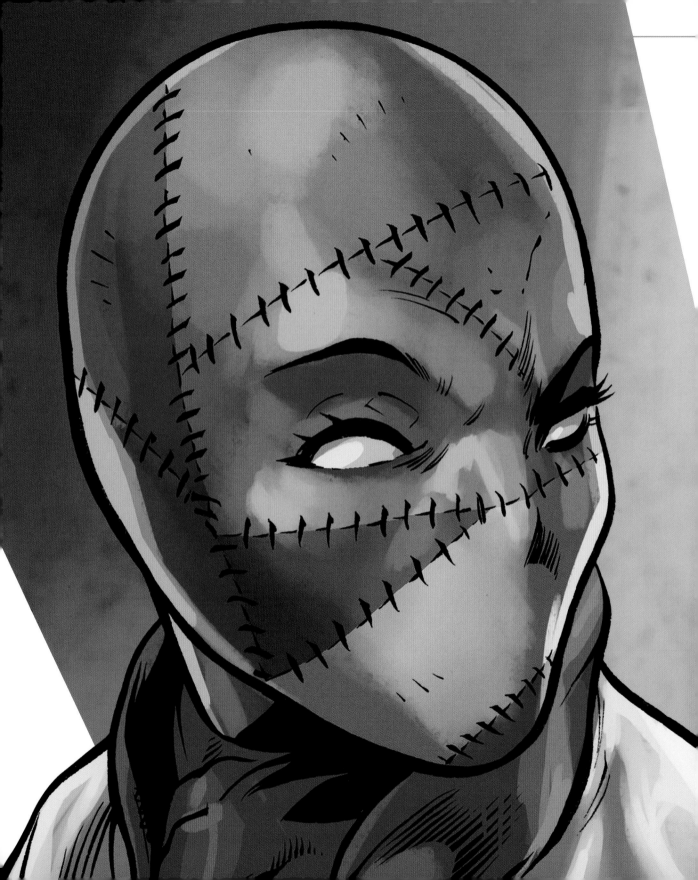

STITCH

They/them

"Fate sent me to this school to learn how to be a hero. But really? I just came here to find my people."

Stitch is a magically animated ragdoll who works as an apprentice to a Super Hero wizard named Doctor Fate. Upon recognizing the heroic soul within the mismatched patches, Doctor Fate encouraged his protégé to join Titans Academy.

Although Stitch often wishes they were made of stronger stuff than cotton and thread, they have no problem making their feelings known whenever they see injustice, and will stand up to students and teachers alike. After using their powers to save some of their cohorts during a school fight, Stitch's popularity soared and they were elected class president.

Stitch's magical abilities are as varied as the colors of their fabric body—they can move and manipulate objects through the air, create flowers out of nothing, project astral forms, and create an invisibility field. While they may be constructed from the humblest of materials, it is clear that this nonbinary being is built from what heroes are made of.

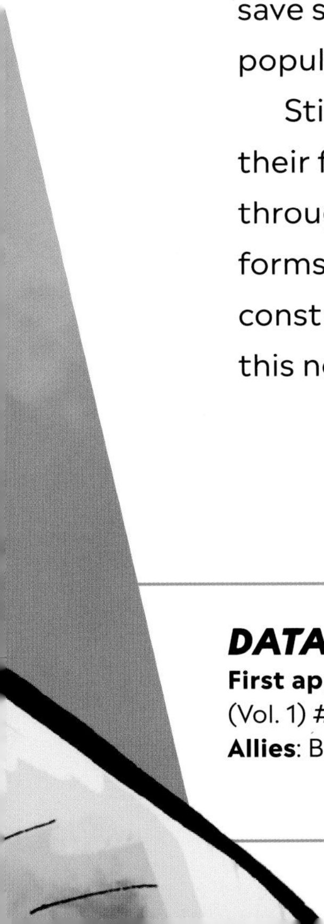

DATA FILE

First appearance: *Teen Titans Academy* (Vol. 1) #1 (2021)

Allies: Bunker, Chupacabra, Matt Price

Likes: Hoodies, peonies, snooping

Dislikes: Matches, lighters, torches—fire of any kind, really

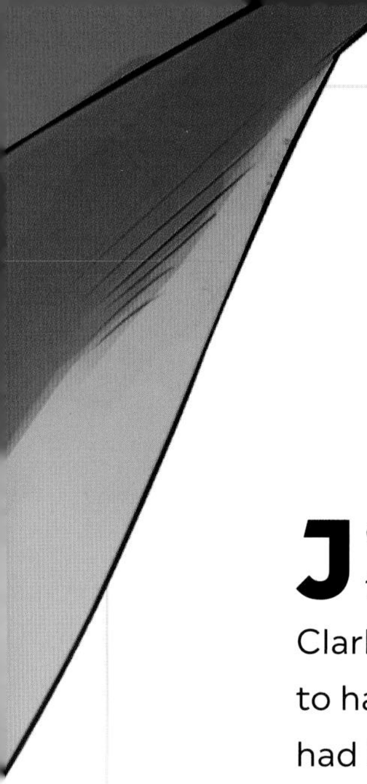

SUPERMAN
(JON KENT)

He/him

"Truth. Justice. And a better world."

Jonathan "Jon" Kent lived the first years of his life unaware that his parents were acclaimed journalist Lois Lane and Clark Kent, the original Superman. Clark and Lois wanted him to have a normal childhood, but when they realized that Jon had inherited Clark's powers, it became clear that their son was too extraordinary to ever be ordinary.

Wearing his own version of his father's costume, 10-year-old Jon had a brief but eventful career as Superboy, frequently teaming up with Batman's son, Damian Wayne. It was during one of these Superboy adventures that Jon found himself trapped on an alternate Earth and spent seven long years trying to get home. When he finally made it back, he discovered that on his Earth, he had only been gone for three weeks!

As a teenager, Superboy continued to fight evil at his father's side. When Clark had to go to space and deal with an intergalactic threat, Jon took up the mantle of Superman, determined to live up to his father's name. Jon also began exploring his bisexuality and started dating Jay Nakamura. Jon was nervous about his father's reaction to his boyfriend, but he needn't have worried. Clark returned home with nothing but love and acceptance.

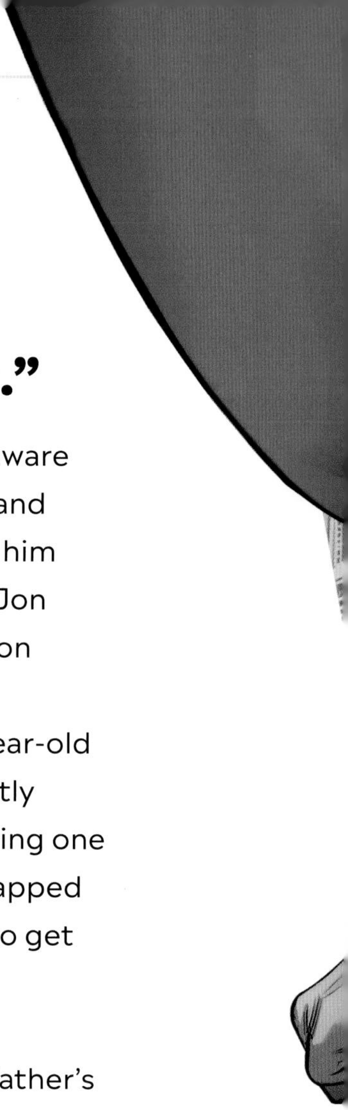

DATA FILE

First appearance: *Convergence: Superman* (Vol. 1) #2 (2015)
Allies: Robin (Damian Wayne), Superman (Clark Kent), Jay Nakamura, Dreamer, The Aerie, Wink, Aquaman (Jackson Hyde)
Base: Metropolis
Likes: Learning new languages, driving tractors, his beat-up red SUV

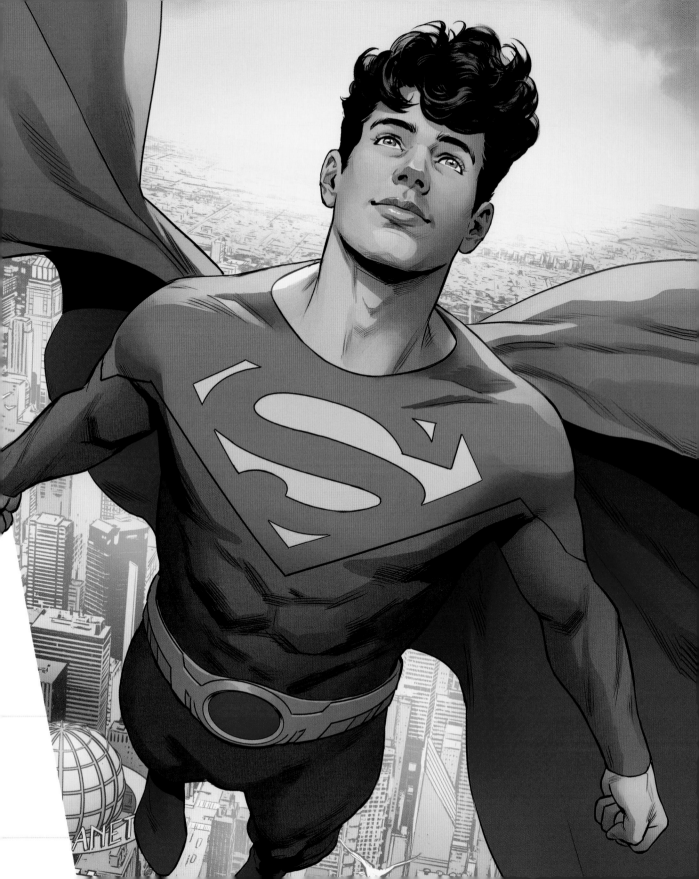

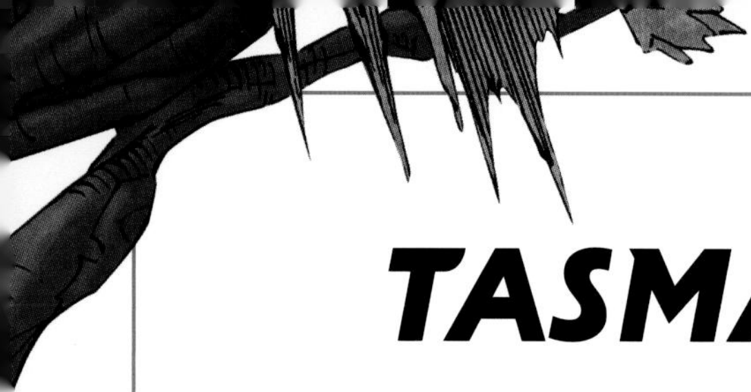

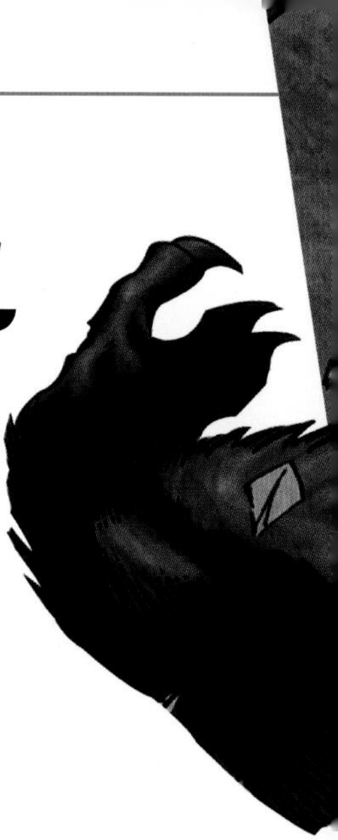

TASMANIAN DEVIL

He/him

"You drongos will have to do better than that if you want to beat the devil!"

It's difficult to get a straight answer out of Hugh Dawkins. When asked about the origin of his ability to transform into a hulking, furry dynamo with claws sharp enough to rend steel, Australia's most famous Super Hero prefers to joke. Hugh has said that his mother was a were-Tasmanian devil, who raised him in a cult that worships the Tasmanian devil. She then gave him a Tasmanian devil amulet and sold his soul to a devil who resided in Tasmania, but only after injecting him with radioactive Tasmanian devil musk that came from a race of alien Tasmanian devils! Clearly, Hugh was having some fun.

But while his origins are obscured by jokes and wisecracks, Hugh has never hidden his sexuality. He has the distinction of being the first openly gay man in the Justice League. After a long relationship with Mikaal Thomas, a.k.a. Starman, Hugh has since settled down and married Gregorio de la Vega, the wizard known as Extraño, and together they are raising their daughter, Suri.

DATA FILE

First appearance: *Infinity Inc.* (Vol. 1) #32 (1986)
Allies: Extraño, Starman (Mikaal Thomas), Midnighter
Likes: Volleyball, fried John Dory, reality TV series
Dislikes: Sunburn, Australian-themed steakhouse chains, drongos

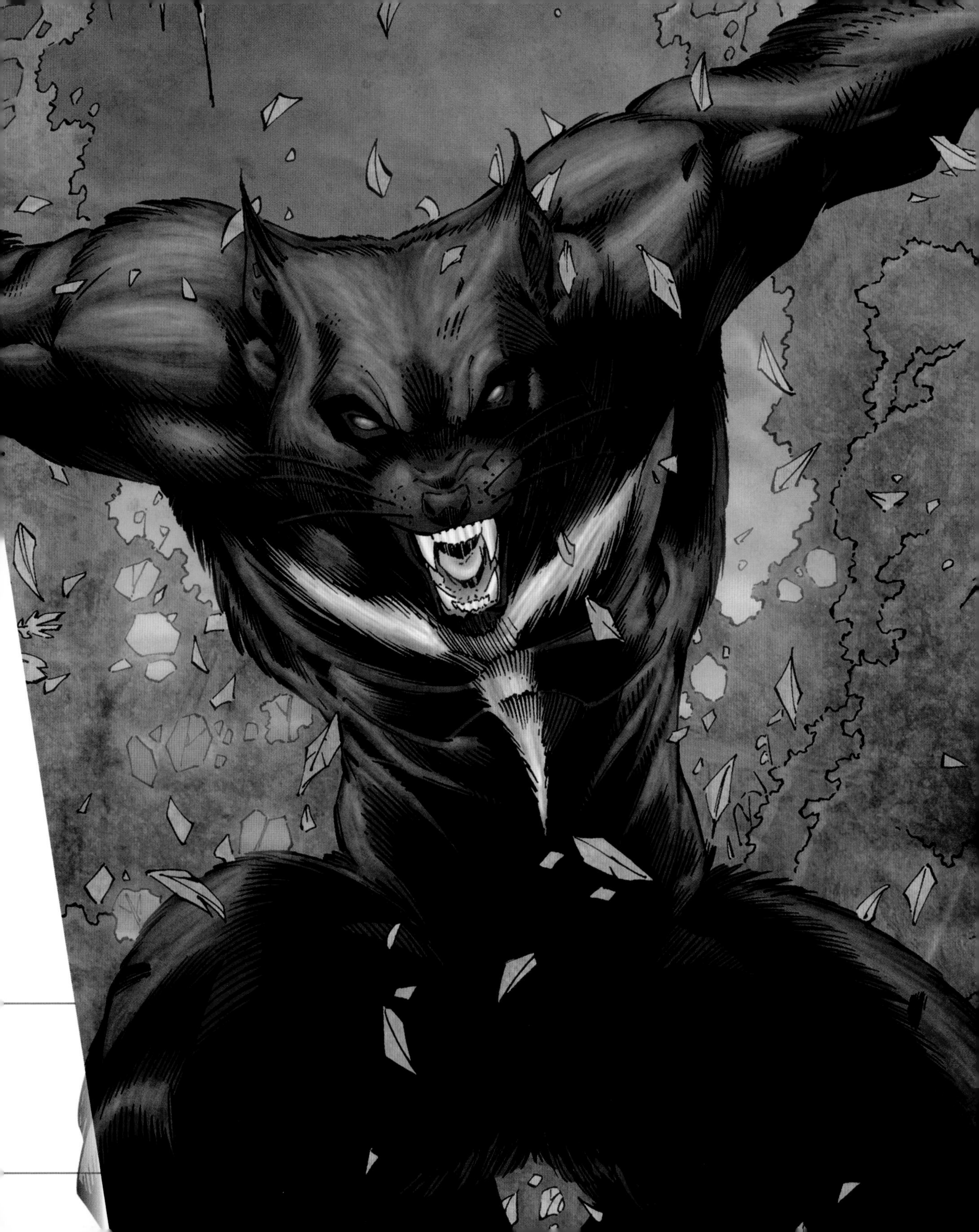

TERRY BERG

He/him

"I'm not going to lie about it.
This is who I am."

Terry Berg was never a Super Hero—but he has the heart of one. A talented artist, he interned at Feast magazine, where he assisted cartoonist Kyle Rayner, a.k.a. the Super Hero Green Lantern. Terry's job was to make sure Kyle's popular "City Dwellers" comic strip was completed on time—something Kyle had trouble with, as he was frequently called away from his drawing table to save the galaxy.

Kyle was the first person to whom Terry came out as gay. When that conversation went well, Terry decided to open up about his sexuality to his mother and friends at school, too. Unfortunately, the rest of the people in his life did not respond as positively as Kyle, and Terry found himself a social outcast—first kicked out of his parents' home, then assaulted by a homophobic gang.

But Terry's fighting spirit never diminished. When he recovered from his injuries, he moved in with his boyfriend, David, and devoted his energy to anti-hate-crime activism and writing books about his life experiences. Terry remains a close friend and confidante of Kyle Rayner—once even convincing the Green Lantern not to abandon Earth during a dark time.

DATA FILE
First appearance: *Green Lantern* (Vol. 3) #129 (2000)
Aliases: T-Berg, Superstar

Likes: Hi-res monitors, band T-shirts
Dislikes: Drawing things with ink, small dogs

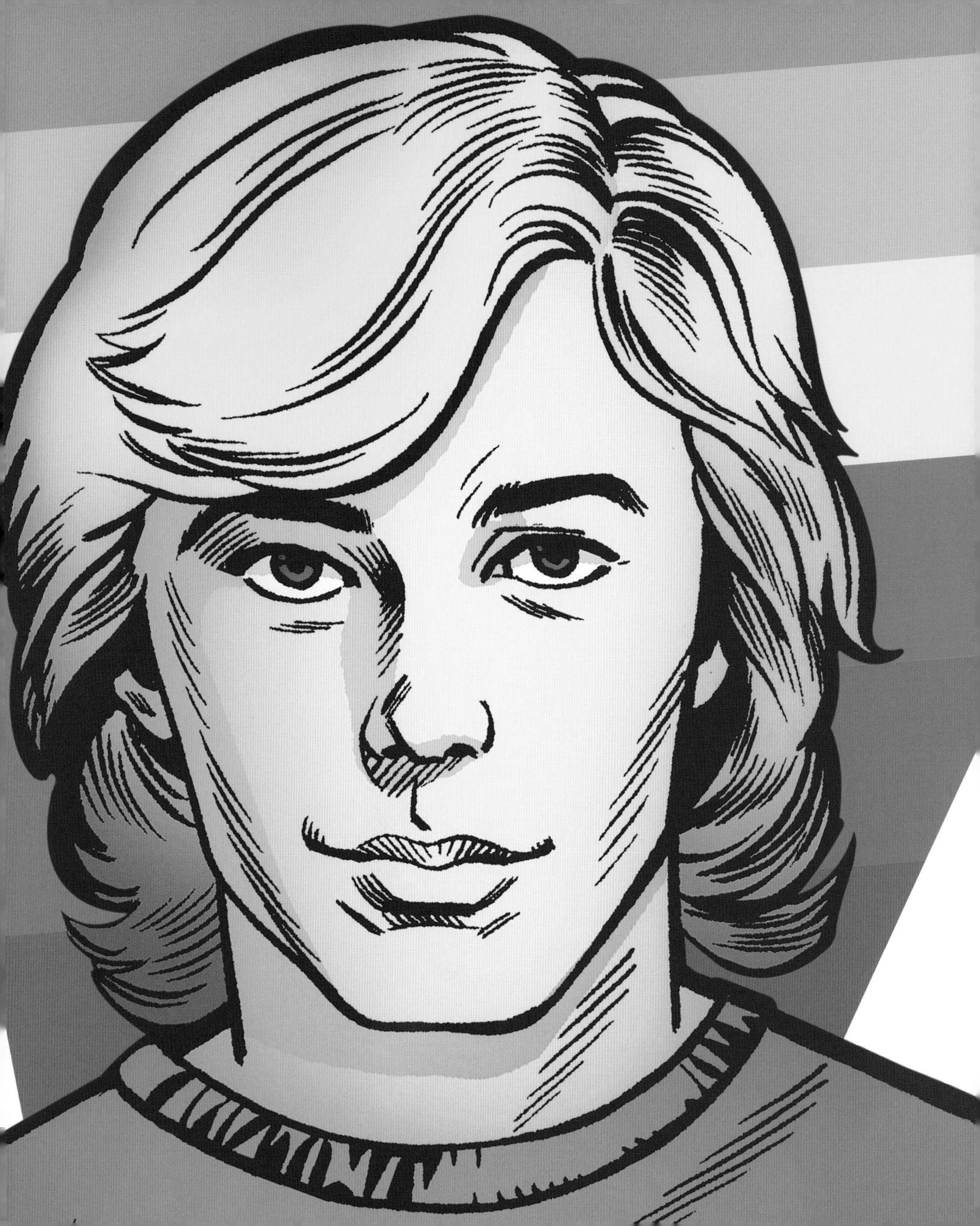

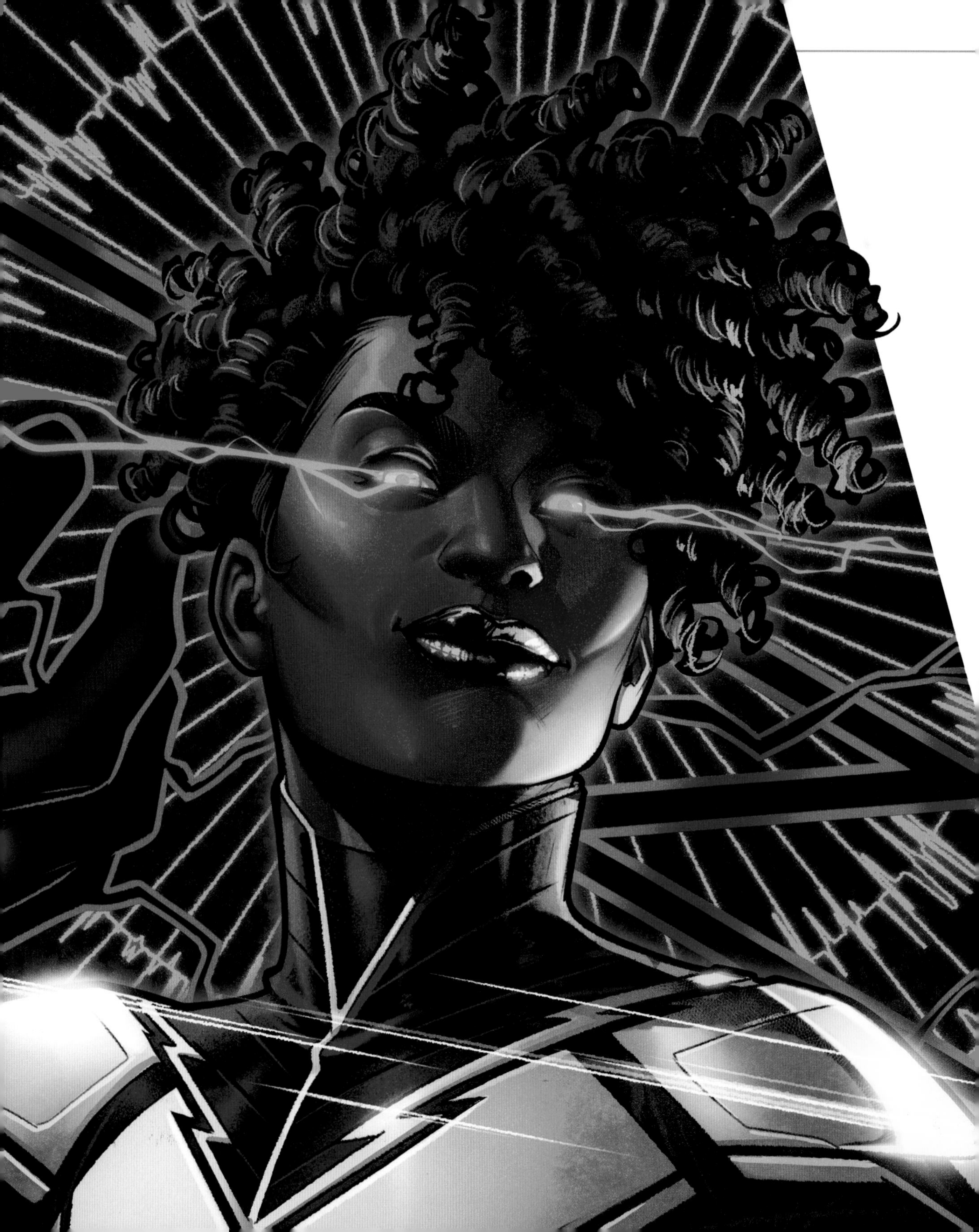

THUNDER

She/her

"We fought **in honor** of those who came before us, and **in obligation** to the generations yet to come."

Anissa Pierce, daughter of the Super Hero Black Lightning, was born with the ability to increase the density of her body, making her super strong and almost impossible to harm. Anissa promised her father she wouldn't become a Super Hero until after college, and she kept her word—just. The very second graduation was over, Anissa began her vigilante career as Thunder!

Anissa joined the Batman-led Super Hero team the Outsiders, where she met and immediately developed an argumentative relationship with her teammate Grace Choi. The fights belied simmering romantic tensions. Anissa had known she was a lesbian since high school, but remained in the closet until her feelings for Grace overwhelmed her fears. Once their relationship blossomed, Anissa always stood by Grace, even after Batman kicked Anissa off the team for her lack of ruthlessness.

In the end, Anissa chose to live a quiet life with Grace. But when adventure finds its way to her doorstep, she is ready to step up for those she swore to defend.

DATA FILE

First appearance: *Outsiders* (Vol. 3) #1 (2003)
Allies: Grace Choi, Black Lightning, Lightning, Nightwing, Arsenal, Shift

Likes: Television. LOTS of television
Dislikes: Being told what to do, cilantro

TRACI 13

She/her

"Magic doesn't usually come with happy endings."

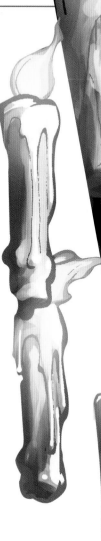

Growing up, Traci 13 found herself caught between two worlds. Her father was the renowned skeptic Doctor Thirteen, while her mother was the fabled sorceress Meihui Lan, who taught Traci magic in secret. When Meihui Lan disappeared in the midst of a great battle with the dark forces Doctor Thirteen refused to believe in, her father forbade Traci from practicing magic.

In spite of her father's ruling, the young mage didn't stop using the gifts her mother has passed down to her. Though estranged from Doctor Thirteen, Traci soon found people who appreciated her magic, and she has since helped super-teams such as the Teen Titans, Night Force, and Justice League Dark fight supernatural evils. Sometimes the mage even finds herself tangled up romantically with the Super Heroes she's helped, most notably Blue Beetle (Jaime Reyes) and Steel (Natasha Irons).

Traci used her magical abilities to set up shop in Metropolis, advertising herself as a supernatural problem solver. As one of the most powerful mages in the world, she has also created her own society, the Sisterhood of the Sleight Hand, who offer help to mortal heroes in need.

DATA FILE

First appearance: *Superman* (Vol. 2) #189 (2003)
Allies: Steel (Natasha Irons), Superwoman, Raven, Blue Beetle (Jaime Reyes)

Likes: Streetlights, the high-pitched song of the subway
Dislikes: Demons, trying on shoes, waiting in line

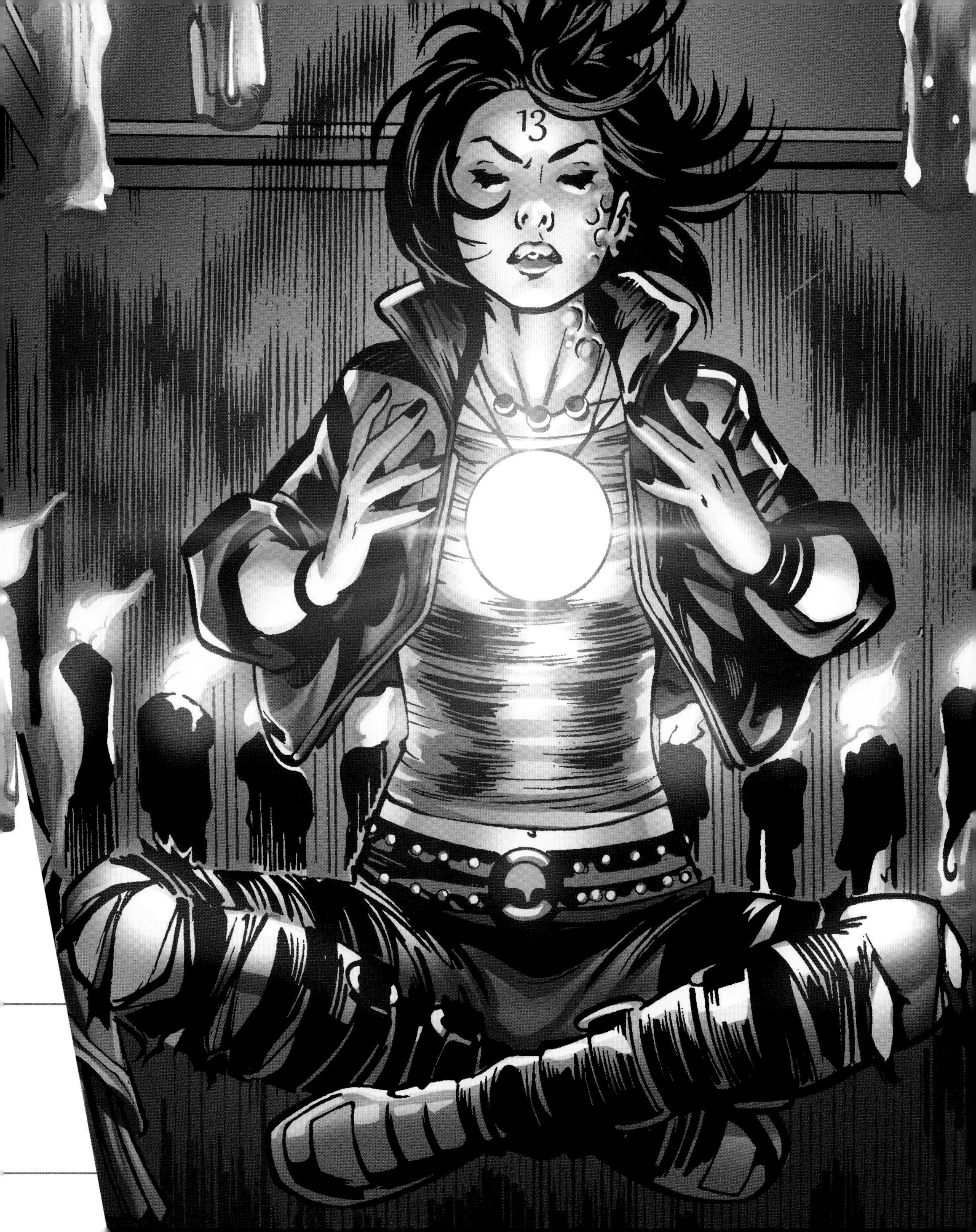
13

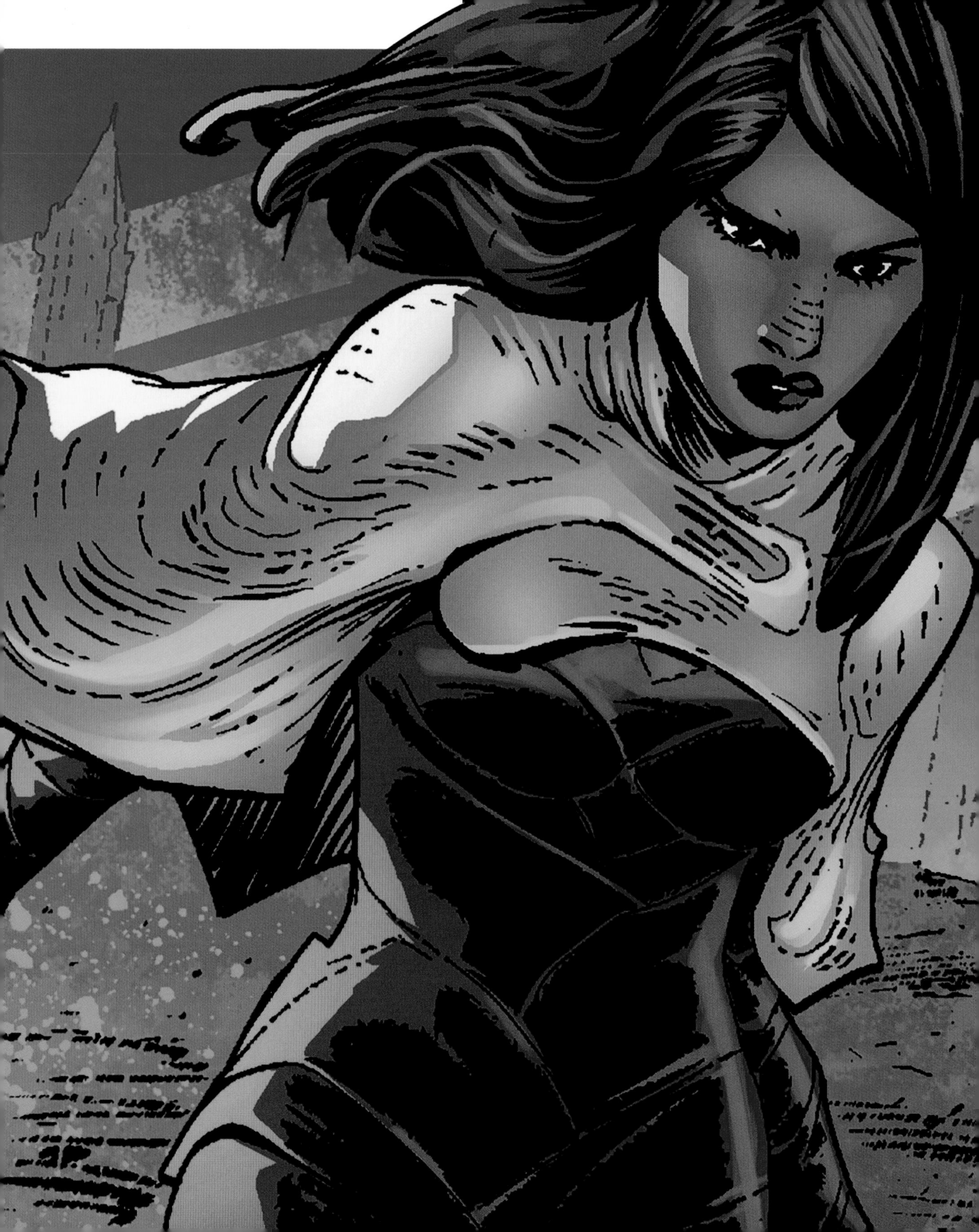

TREMOR

She/her

"If you don't want your hand liquefied, don't touch me again without permission. Is that clear?"

Roshanna Chatterji's life changed forever when she discovered she had the ability to create shockwaves in the earth. While she was happy to display these powers for her whole village to see, these acts only led to accusations of being a witch.

Hoping for a fresh start, Roshanna moved from India to America—only to find herself amidst a group of girls just as troubled as she herself felt. When Roshanna awoke from a tragic accident to discover she was the only survivor, she avoided prison by working for a government agent named Amanda Waller. Roshanna was given a costumed secret identity—Tremor—and ordered to pose as a Super-Villain and recruit members of the Secret Six. When that mission ended, Waller sent her out once more—this time as a supposedly reformed hero with the objective to infiltrate and inform on ragtag Super Hero team The Movement.

Eventually, Roshanna grew tired of lying to people she had come to trust, so chose to break her ties with the manipulative Waller. Since then, she has been open about her asexuality with her teammates and is now ready to show everyone who she really is.

DATA FILE

First Appearance: *Secret Six* (Vol. 3) #25 (2013)
Allies: Virtue, Vengeance Moth

Likes: Tea, thin-tipped liquid eyeliner, apricots
Dislikes: Assumptions, Amanda Waller

VICTORIA OCTOBER

She/her

"Welcome to my evil lair."

In a world filled with scientific innovation and evil geniuses, Dr. Victoria October stands apart from the rest. This brilliant scientist swiftly rose through the ranks at the government agency A.R.G.U.S., becoming the leading authority on biological weapons. Neither evil nor entirely noble in her intentions, Victoria's only concern is using her skills to make living as a human easier. In her eyes, focusing on things like morality is a waste of time.

Batman and Batwoman (Kate Kane) came to trust this determined scientist, and Victoria became one of the few people outside of the Batman Family allowed access to the hi-tech Belfry base in Gotham City. Since becoming Batman's ally, she has helped solve several cases—from dealing with Professor Hugo Strange's monster serum to finding a cure to help shape-shifting Bat-Family member Clayface.

A transgender woman and lesbian, Victoria believes that transitioning opened her eyes to the myriad possibilities the world could offer. Bodies can change, love is too broad to define, and science can make one's wildest dreams and most terrible nightmares come true.

DATA FILE

First appearance: *Detective Comics* (Vol. 1) #948 (2017)
Allies: Batman, Batwoman (Kate Kane), Robin (Tim Drake)

Likes: Pho, knee-high boots, black-and-white movies
Dislikes: Dirty tools, lack of citations, iced tea made from a powder

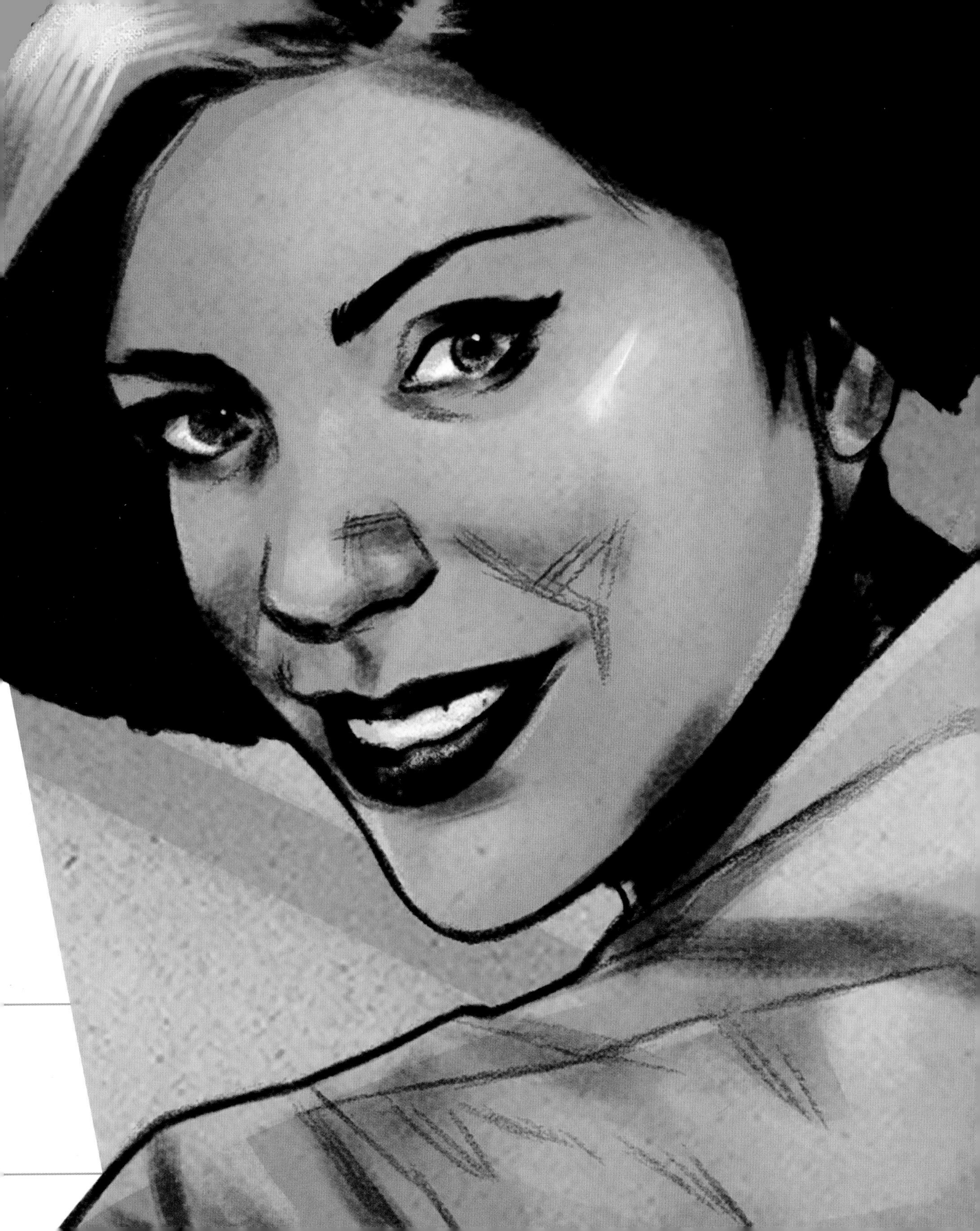

WINK

She/her

"Gasp. A last minute rescue! Who could have foreseen such an eventuality?"

Wink has trouble with boundaries—especially staying within them. When she was abducted and experimented on by the illegal Post-Human Project, Wink gained the ability to teleport. She kept this superpower hidden from her captors, regularly leaving her cell without them knowing.

Although Wink couldn't teleport far, she was able to enter the cell where her fellow prisoner The Aerie was kept, and a relationship bloomed between them. The couple managed to escape their imprisonment, and soon joined a superpowered activist team, The Revolutionaries. Wink believed in what The Revolutionaries stood for and helped them attack corrupt government organizations like the one that had kidnapped her.

After a difficult stint as reluctant members of the Suicide Squad, Wink and The Aerie returned to their life of activism with The Revolutionaries, and later joined Jay Nakamura's group The Truth. In a world filled with uncertainty, this queer woman knows two things to be true—she loves The Aerie, and no one is going to put her in a cage ever again.

DATA FILE

First appearance: *Suicide Squad* (Vol. 6) #1 (2020)
Allies: The Aerie, Jay Nakamura, Superman (Jon Kent), Harley Quinn

Likes: Batman, The Flash, taking things that don't belong to her
Dislikes: Submarines, authority, cages

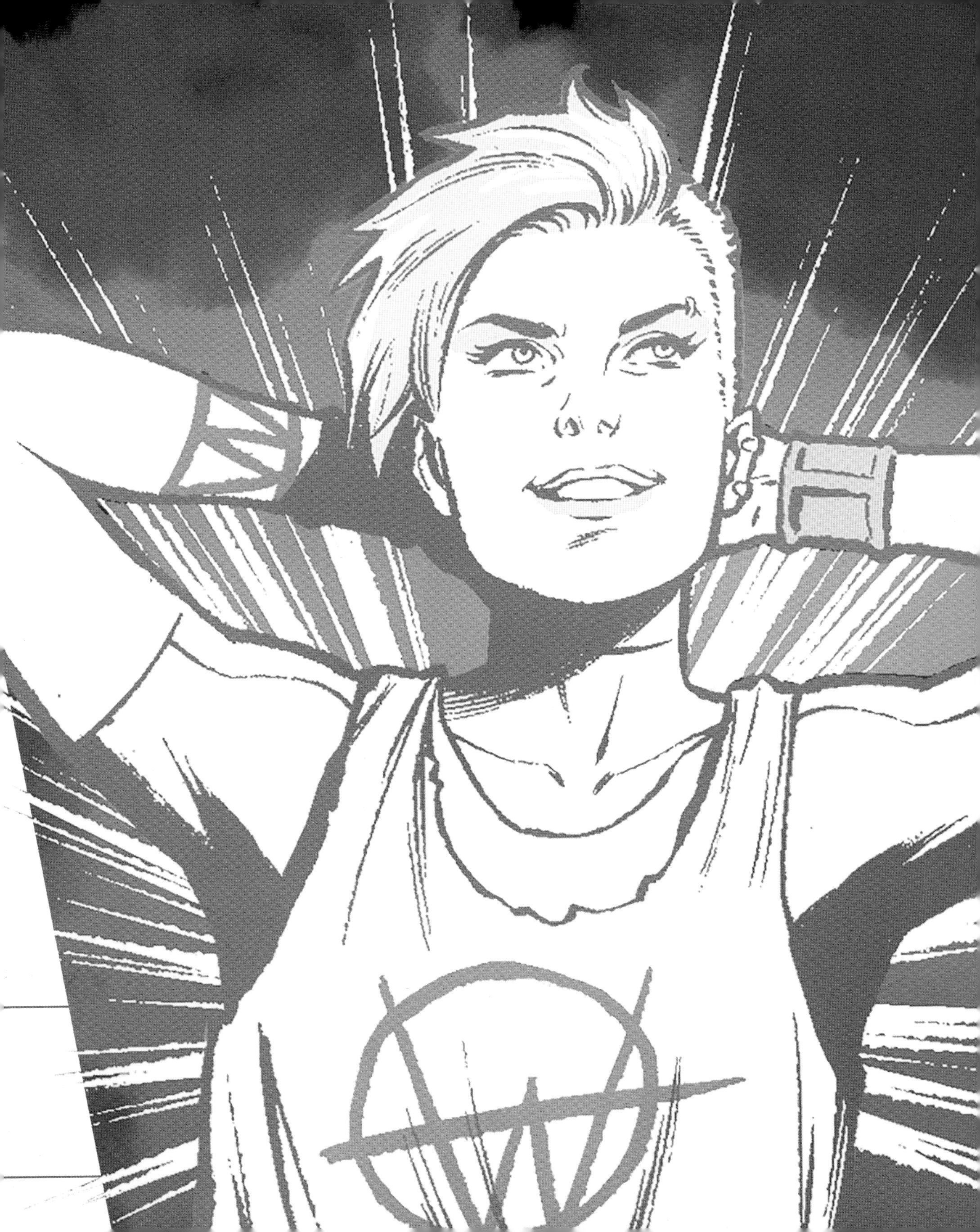

GLOSSARY

Aromantic: Describes a person who does not experience romantic attraction to others. An aromantic person is not necessarily asexual, just as an asexual person is not necessarily aromantic.

Asexual: Describes a person who does not experience sexual attraction or is not interested in sexual activity with others. Asexuality exists on a spectrum, and asexual people may experience no, little, or conditional sexual attraction.

Bisexual: Describes a person emotionally, romantically, or sexually attracted to more than one gender though not necessarily in the same way or to the same degree.

Gay: Describes a person who is emotionally, romantically, or sexually attracted to members of the same gender. Men, women, and non-binary people use this term to describe themselves, but it is most commonly associated with men.

Genderfluid: Describes a person whose gender identity or expression shifts.

Genderqueer: Describes a person whose gender identity is neither a man nor a woman, is between or beyond genders, or is some combination of genders.

Green Lantern: A member of the intergalactic police force, the Green Lantern Corps, organized by the Guardians of the Universe. Each Green Lantern is responsible for a sector of the galaxy and is given a power ring, which allows them to manipulate green energy directed by their willpower.

Guardians of the Universe: A group of immortal aliens from the planet Oa, who created and oversee the Green Lantern Corps.

Intersex: Describes bodies that fall outside society's definitions of male and female. There are lots of ways someone can be intersex.

Lesbian: Describes a woman who is emotionally, romantically, or sexually attracted to other women. The term is also used by some non-binary people who are attracted to women.

LGBTQIA+: An acronym commonly used to refer to Lesbian, Gay, Bisexual, Transgender, Queer and/or Questioning, Intersex, and Asexual and/or Aromantic individuals and communities.

Metahuman: Describes a person who possesses superpowers.

Non-binary: Describes a person whose gender identity is not just male or female all of the time. Words that people may use to express their non-binary gender identity include "genderqueer" and "genderfluid."

Queer: Queer is used as a catch-all term for people whose emotional, romantic, or sexual attraction includes people of the same gender. It is also used by non-binary or gender-expansive people.

Questioning: A term used to describe people who are in the process of exploring their sexual orientation or gender identity.

Speed Force: A cosmic force that is the representation of reality in motion. A person tapping into the Speed Force can move with incredible velocity.

Teen Titans: A Super Hero team whose membership consists of teenage heroes.

Teen Titans Academy: A school for training the next members of the Teen Titans.

GLOSSARY (CONTINUED)

Themyscira: The island nation of the immortal Amazons. Also called "Paradise Island."

Trans: Describes a person whose gender identity is not aligned with the sex they were assigned at birth. "Trans" is an umbrella term to refer to the full range and diversity of identities within transgender communities.

The Truth: An international group of activists fighting for justice. They run a website, also called The Truth, where they publish stories the mainstream media does not.

Well of Souls: A place where the souls of women who died through acts of violence reside. These souls are reborn to new bodies as Amazons of Themyscira.

ARTIST ACKNOWLEDGMENTS

Juan Albarran, Oclair Albert, Ulises Arreola, Jadzia Axelrod, Vita Ayala, Darryl Banks, David Baron, Jen Bartel, Moose Baumann, Jordie Bellaire, Brian Michael Bendis, Marguerite Bennett, Federico Blee, Tamra Bonvillain, Sweeney Boo, Ted Brandt, Chuck Brown, Ed Brubaker, Stephen Byrne, Evan Cagle, Jamal Campbell, Mauro Cascioli, Derek Charm, Sebastian Cheng, Michael Cho, Becky Cloonan, Ivan Cohen, Michael W. Conrad, Paul Cornell, Jeromy Cox, Andrew Dalhouse, Tom Derenick, Romulo Fajardo, Jr., Ray Fawkes, Meghan Fitzmartin, Travel Foreman, Eduardo Francisco, Gary Frank, Crystal Frasier, Richard Friend, Juan Gedeon, Patrick Gleason, Sina Grace, Stephanie Hans, Hi-Fi Design, Kyle Higgins, Jamison, Mikel Janín, N.K. Jemisin, Jorge Jiménez, Geoff Johns, Dave Johnson, Phillip Kennedy Johnson, A.L. Kaplan, Stanley Lau, John Layman, InHyuk lee, Jeff Lemire, Scott Lobdell, Rex Lokus, Emilio Lopez, Danny Lore, Adriano Lucas, Nicole Maines, Marcelo Maiolo, Guy Major, Francis Manapul, Alitha Martinez, Jesús Merino, Travis Moore, Dan Mora, Mark Morales, Tomeu Morey, Grant Morrison, Juliet Nneka, Rex Ogle, Steve Oliff, Ben Oliver, Steve Orlando, Fico Ossio, Roland Paris, Allen Passalaqua, Jason Paz, Scott Peterson, Joe Phillips, Rachel Pollack, Howard Porter, Christopher Priest, Joe Quinones, Ben Raab, Norm Rapmund, Bruno Redondo, Stefani Rennee, Dinei Ribeiro, John Ridley, David Roach, Darick Robertson, James Robinson, Greg Rucka, Alejandro Sánchez, Nicola Scott, Tim Seeley, Kelsey Shannon, Andrea Shea, Tim Sheridan, Gail Simone, Alex Sinclair, Scott Snyder, Chris Sotomayor, John Stanisci, Ro Stein, Cameron Stewart, Dave Stewart, Tom Sutton, Marcio Takara, David Talaski, Mariko Tamaki, Jordi Tarragona, Jess Taylor, Rick Taylor, Tom Taylor, Art Thibert, Brandon Thomas, Cian Tormey, James Tynion IV, Luciano Vecchio, Wade Von Grawbadger, Mark Waid, Andrew Wheeler, Freddie E. Williams II, Stephanie Williams, Joshua Williamson, G. Willow Wilson, Judd Winick, Pete Woods, Jason Wright, Xermanico, Lynne Yoshii, Tom Ziuko

The publishers have made every effort to identify and acknowledge the artists whose work appears in this book.

Penguin Random House

Senior Editor Matt Jones
Project Art Editor Chris Gould
Editor Frankie Hallam
Production Editor Marc Staples
Senior Production Controller Mary Slater
Managing Editor Emma Grange
Managing Art Editor Vicky Short
Publishing Director Mark Searle

Edited for DK by Lauren Nesworthy
Designed for DK by Jim Green
Cover artist Paulina Ganucheau

DK would like to thank Benjamin Harper at Warner Bros. Consumer Products; Andrea Shea, Doug Prinzivalli, Brittany Holzherr, Dave Weilgosz, Jillian Grant, Arianna Turturro, Jessica Berbey, Chris Conory, Steve Sonn, Leah Tuttle, Hank Manfra, and Benjamin Le Clear at DC; Colin Williams for design assistance; Cefn Ridout for editorial assistance; Megan Douglass for proofreading and americanization; Meg Humphries for proofreading; Kit Heyam for providing the authenticity read; DK's Diversity, Equity, and Inclusion Group for their advice and assistance; and Paulina Ganucheau and Jadzia Axelrod.

Author's Acknowledgments
This book could not have existed without the tireless efforts of my research assistants Alex Jaffe, Zoe Tunnell, Carol Anne Brennaman, Chris Ceary, and Jolene Z, or the endless patience and grace of my wife, JR. Blackwell, and my mother-in-law, Kae Kalwaic. The deepest, most heartfelt thanks to all of you, my own personal Justice League.

First American Edition, 2023
Published in the United States by DK Publishing
1745 Broadway, 20th Floor, New York, NY 10019

Page Design Copyright © 2023 Dorling Kindersley Limited
DK, a Division of Penguin Random House LLC
23 24 25 26 27 10 9 8 7 6 5 4 3 2
002–333494–May/2023

A catalog record for this book
is available from the Library of Congress.
ISBN 978-0-7440-8170-1

DK books are available at special discounts when purchased in bulk for sales promotions, premiums, fund-raising, or educational use. For details, contact: DK Publishing Special Markets, 1745 Broadway, 20th Floor, New York, NY 10019
SpecialSales@dk.com

Printed and bound in China

For the curious

www.dk.com

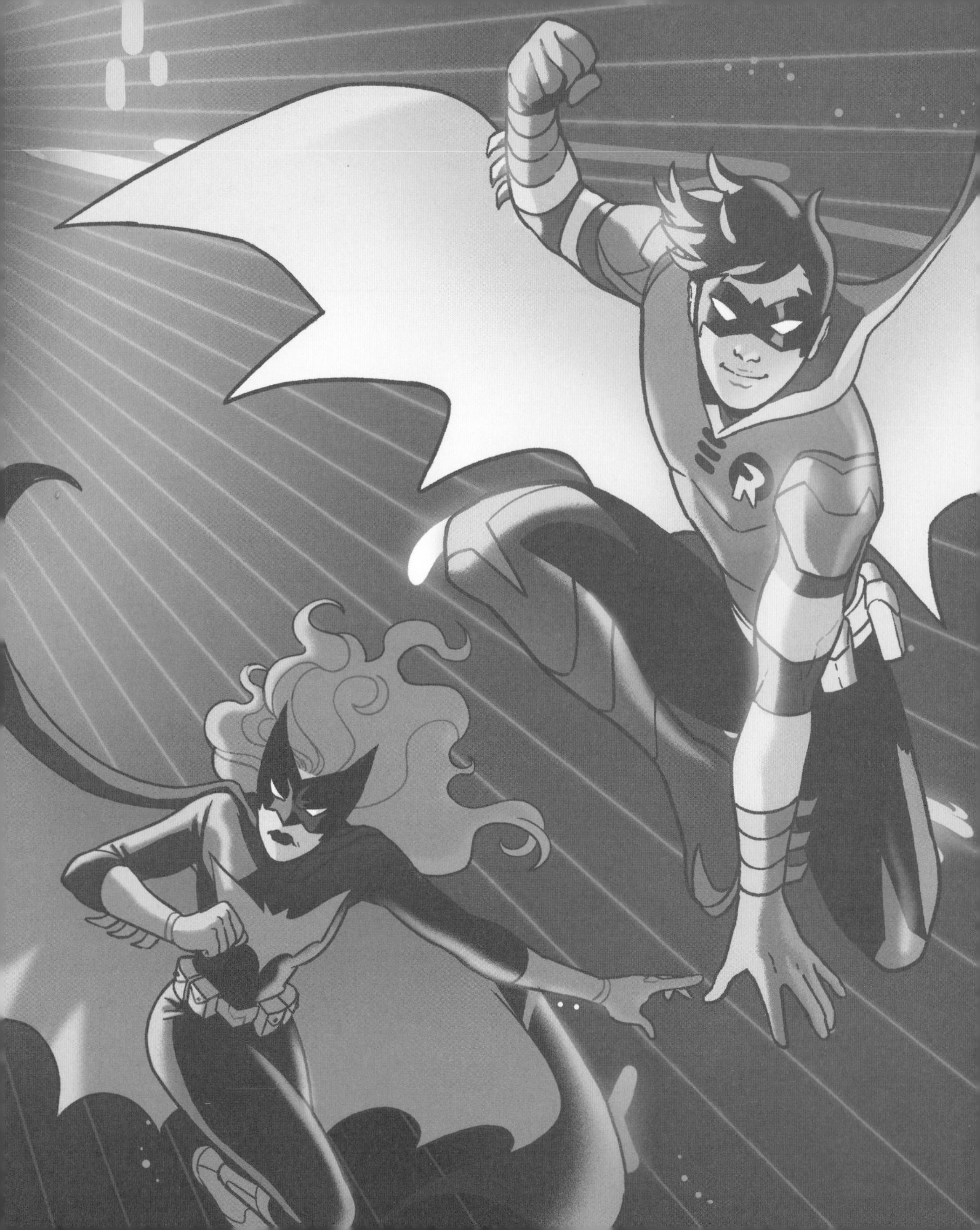